U2

SONG BY SONG

AARON J. SAMS

FONTHILL

Fonthill Media Language Policy

Fonthill Media publishes in the international English language market. One language edition is published worldwide. As there are minor differences in spelling and presentation, especially with regard to American English and British English, a policy is necessary to define which form of English to use. The Fonthill Policy is to use the form of English native to the author. Aaron J. Sams was born and educated in Canada; therefore Canadian English has been adopted in this publication.

Fonthill Media Limited
Fonthill Media LLC
www.fonthill.media
office@fonthillmedia.com

First published in the United Kingdom and the United States of America 2024

British Library Cataloguing in Publication Data:
A catalogue record for this book is available from the British Library

Copyright © Aaron J. Sams 2024

ISBN 978-1-78155-899-7

Typeset in 10pt on 13pt Sabon
Printed and bound in England

Acknowledgements

Since I discovered U2 at the age of ten, back in 1983, I have not really looked back. But writing a book like this forces you to look back. At that age, in a small town in Eastern Canada, without even a record shop, I could not imagine where my love of this band would take me. But I could dream big. I dreamed about seeing the world, about seeing this band I love, and yes, even then I wanted to write a book someday.

In 1995 I took a computer class and was challenged to pick a topic I loved to become a website. I picked U2. That was the start of the site that operates as U2Songs.com now, the oldest U2 fan site that has been in continuous operation since that time.

The website and associated projects have introduced me to so many other fans. This book would not have happened without those fans who have lifted me up over the years. I cannot begin to name names, as I would leave someone out, but you know who you are—you have shared hotels, traded tickets, sat on sidewalks in the middle of the night with me, and many of you have become like family to me.

I do have to thank several people who directly contributed to the book you hold in your hands. Dan Basquill, Karl Blain, Stefanie Bowen, Patty Culliton, Tim Cunningham, Naomi Dinnen, Dan Eliot, Chris Flahaven, Alexander Fraga Gomez, Brad Hood, Alan Ivory, Harry Kantas, Karin King, Mike Long, Paul Lunn, Amra Merdanovic, Don Morgan, Jim Parker, Don Patterson, Gary Paul, Scott Peretta, Shawn Rocco, Nicole Sansonetti, Carl Uebelhart, and Caroline van Oosten de Boer—many thanks for what you have added here.

I do not need to tell anyone what these songs mean. We all find our own meanings within the songs. But I have included several comments from U2 themselves which may lead you down a path. I have had many opportunities because of this band. My life is considerably different than what it would have been without them. For the friendships your band has spawned, the travel, the amazing shows, and the amazing songs, many thanks.

Thank you to U2's fans for sharing stories and sharing your love.

Thank you to Jay Slater at Fonthill Media who reached out to myself and Harry Kantas when looking for an author for this book.

Thanks to my dad, Angus, Madelyn, Adam, and Alison. You may not have understood this journey at times, but you always supported it. And a huge thanks to Paul. This book could not have been done without your patience and support.

This book is dedicated to my mother, Linda. She took me to my first big concert, she told me to dream big, and she always told me someday I would write a book.

Contents

Introduction

U2 formed in 1976 when a bunch of school kids got together in Larry Mullen's kitchen on Rosemount Avenue after Mullen had posted a note to the school bulletin board asking if anyone wanted to start a band. The band first met on September 25, 1976. Initially they tried out a few names, such as Feedback and then The Hype, before choosing U2 as a name.

When they settled on a name, they also settled on a line up, and since 1977, U2 has consisted of Bono (lead vocals, guitar, harmonica), Edge (guitar, keyboards, backing vocals), Larry Mullen (drums, percussion, some vocals), and Adam Clayton (bass guitar). They have maintained the same line up over the years, and only have occasionally played with any member missing.

The band signed to CBS Records in Ireland, a contract covering their first four albums. Four years after forming, they signed a worldwide contract with Island Records, a relationship which continues to this day.

The band have been nominated for forty-seven Grammy Awards and have won twenty-two, more than any other band. U2 have won two Golden Globe Awards for songs they contributed to *Gangs of New York* and *Mandela: Long Walk to Freedom*. In 2001 they were given the Outstanding Contribution to Music Award at the Brit Awards. They have even won an Emmy Award at the Sports Emmys in 2011 for their FIFA World Cup ad with the Soweto Gospel Choir. In 2005 they were inducted into the Rock and Roll Hall of Fame. In 2016 they were awarded the Innovator Award at the iHeart Music Awards.

The band are not only known for their songs, but also for their ground-breaking tours. The band are always pushing forward technology in a live setting to get closer to their audiences. The U2360° Tour in 2009–2011 set worldwide box office records, including Highest Grossing tour, a record they held until 2019.

Throughout their career, U2 have used their voice to improve human rights and have been involved in several charitable organizations. Early contributions included work with Amnesty International and Special Olympics. In the 1990s the band got involved in human rights for gays and lesbians and AIDS charities, including contributions to the *Out Loud* and *Red Hot and Blue* compilations, and contributing all royalties from their single "One" to AIDS research. In the 2000s Bono was instrumental in campaigning for debt relief as well as for AIDS in Africa, starting organizations such as DATA, (RED), and One. The band has also been involved in obtaining musical instruments and opportunities for children through organizations such as Music Rising, Music Generation, and Education through Music. They have also been involved in organization such as Greenpeace, Mencap, and Stand Up to Cancer.

In their forty-six-year career, U2 have released fourteen full-length albums, and an additional album featuring the entire band under the name Passengers. They have released over seventy singles throughout their career. This book will examine each officially released song from these albums and singles in detail, from the earliest songs to the most recent.

1

Boy (1980)

Boy was U2's first full-length album, recorded between July and September 1980 with producer Steve Lillywhite. Originally the band had approached Martin Hannett to produce the album, but when Ian Curtis of Joy Division took his own life, Hannett was reluctant to take the role. U2 had concerns that working with a superstar producer like Hannett would overshadow their work, so parted ways amicably. Lillywhite was working as a staff producer at Island Records and stepped in to join the band in Windmill Lane Studios in Dublin. Several songs on *Boy* had been released earlier, but all were rerecorded with Lillywhite for the album. *Boy* was released October 20, 1980 in Europe. The North American release happened on March 3, 1981.

The cover of *Boy* features a young boy named Peter Rowen, who was a neighbor of Bono's and the little brother of Bono's good friend Guggi. The design of the cover was done by Steve Averill. In North America, the label had concerns about releasing an album by an unknown band with a child on the front cover wearing no visible clothing. A new cover featured images of each member of U2 in silhouette stretched using special effects, was designed in-house by Island Records by Bruno Christian-Tilley, the in-house designer at Island Records.

The album reached #52 on the UK album chart and #63 on the *Billboard* 200. The album has been listed in *Rolling Stone*'s Top 500 list at #417 (both 2003 and 2012). The album won several *Hot Press Magazine* Readers Poll awards in 1981 including Best Debut Album, Best Album Sleeve, and Best Irish Album.

In 2008 *Boy* was remastered under the direction of The Edge and released in a deluxe format with additional tracks. In 2020 to mark the fortieth anniversary of the album, *Boy* was released on white vinyl for the Record Store Day Black Friday event.

"I Will Follow"
Lyrics/Music: U2
Producer: Lillywhite

"I Will Follow" is about Bono's mother, Iris, who had died when he was young.

> I felt a real resentment, because I had never got a chance ... to feel that unconditional
> love a mother has for a child. There was a feeling of that house pulled down on top
> of me, because after the death of my mother that house was no longer a home—it
> was just a house. That's what "I Will Follow" is about. It's a little sketch about that
> unconditional love a mother has for a child.[1]

In concert in 2015, Bono would reveal, "When I wrote it, I thought it was a suicide
note from a kid who wanted to follow his mother to the grave, and then ... I
later learned it's a song written from a mother's point of view, it's a song about
unconditional love."[2]

"I Will Follow" was released multiple times. The first release in 1980 featured a
different photo of Peter Rowen on the sleeve. In 1981 it was released as a single in
North America using the album cover for art. These first releases did not chart in
the UK or USA.

Several live releases followed. In 1982, after a strong TV performance in the
Netherlands, a live version of the song was released. In 1983, a live version from
Under a Blood Red Sky was released to promote the live album. This version
saw U2 hit #81 on the USA Billboard Hot 100 chart. And in 2011 after playing
the Glastonbury Festival for the first time, they released a digital single of "I Will
Follow" and reached #78 on the UK Charts.

U2's first video was "I Will Follow," filmed with U2 playing in studio against
a white background. The album cover is imposed over white areas of the video,
added in post-production. The video was initially filmed for promotion, rather
than for airing on video channels, with "Gloria" being the first video to get heavy
airplay on these channels.

Meiert Avis directed the video and shares:

> I helped Brian Masterson build the music studio that U2 recorded in. When they
> weren't recording, they'd come upstairs to my edit bay. It would be three in the
> morning; I'd be up there playing with images. When it came time to do a video, the
> only person they knew who knew anything about video was me, so then I got to
> shoot it. We got money to shoot their first videos. That's how that all began.[3]

Avis would shoot several videos with U2 during their career.

A slightly different version of the song appeared on *The Last American
Virgin* Soundtrack. Another alternate mix appeared in 2008 on deluxe versions

of *Boy.* And a "Special Edited DJ Version" edited the crowd noise on the live performance from *Under a Blood Red Sky,* so it sounded more like a studio track.

"TWILIGHT"
Lyrics/Music: U2
Producer: Lillywhite

Boy was a mix of songs U2 had developed for years and new songs. "Twilight" was one of these older tracks, developed by U2 long before recording *Boy.* "Twilight" was a B-side on U2's second Irish-only single, "Another Day" and had been recorded as a demo in February 1979. The song was rerecorded with Steve Lillywhite for *Boy.*

"Twilight" was a staple of early performances appearing until the War Tour. It was finally retired after a scattering of appearances in Australia during The Unforgettable Fire Tour. Bono has spoken about the lyrics but rarely gives a clear answer as to what the song is about. One such theory discusses his worries about growing old, "It was a riddle. I can remember being told in school about the change in life and how distressing it can be for old men when they stop functioning. I can remember my nervous laugh…"[4]

After the album was released, they received questions from the press about homosexuality. Bono realized the song could have had other connotations—that of a younger man being approached by an older man. Bono admits, "There is with hindsight, as well as near sight, some unusual content."[5]

"AN CAT DUBH"
Lyrics/Music: U2
Producer: Lillywhite

"An Cat Dubh" is Gaelic for "The Black Cat." Bono uses the cat here "as a symbol of temptation. At first beautiful, the shape, you know, seductive. In the daylight it destroys a bird nest. Not for food, but for enjoyment and at the same time it comes up to you and strokes the side of your leg."[6] Bono has shared that it is a song about relationships, and it was written about a time he had separated from Ali. In concert the song is always tied to the song that follows it on the album, "Into the Heart."

In 2018, the album *Souris Calle* featured Bono on "Message to Souris" reading a poem over of U2's recording of "An Cat Dubh."

"An Cat Dubh" was covered and released as a B-side to the Bravery's "Fearless" single, the same year the band opened for U2 at Croke Park.

"INTO THE HEART"
Lyrics/Music: U2
Producer: Lillywhite

"Into the Heart" flows directly from "An Cat Dubh"—this led to some pressings on CD indexing these as one track, while others seem to disagree where one song stops and the next one ends. U2 combines them, even in concert.

The lyrics are short, Bono speaks about going back to childhood, and staying a while. It is retreat into innocence after the story related in "An Cat Dubh."

The song was played regularly with "An Cat Dubh" until 1984, and then U2 would not play it again in full until 2005's Vertigo tour. Even the most unexpected songs can reappear years later.

"OUT OF CONTROL"
Lyrics/Music: U2
Producer: Lillywhite

"Out of Control" was started on Bono's eighteenth birthday in May 1978. The song developed throughout that year, and in August 1979, it was one of the songs that U2 recorded with Chas de Whalley for their first release, "Three." The song was recorded and mixed at Windmill Studio with de Whalley, but U2 would rerecord the songs with Steve Lillywhite when working on *Boy*. The version recorded with Lillywhite is a much tighter recording, an attempt to capture the live feeling of U2.

Bono said:

> "Out of Control" is about waking up on your eighteenth birthday and realizing that you're 18 years old and that the two most important decisions in your life have nothing to do with you—being born and dying. The song is from the child's point of view and it's about a vicious cycle. He becomes a delinquent, but the psychologist says, "it's in his childhood." No matter what he does—it can't be because he wants to, it's always because of what went before and there's no decision in anything. Then again, that's slightly spiritual—the question what is happening if you've no freedom?[7]

"Three" featured "Out of Control," voted on by listeners of Dave Fanning's radio show to be the lead song. The song was released in a special limited 1,000 copy 12-inch record, hand numbered, leading U2 to chart success in Ireland, reaching #19 on the Irish charts. The single was reissued many times on 12-inch, 7-inch, coloured vinyl variations, and on cassette single.

Many recent releases such as the reissue of *Boy* in 2008, *The Complete U2* and the fortieth anniversary reissue of "Three" claim to have the original single version of the song, but this is not the case. On these newer recordings the drums start out with high hats, sounding very different when they come in than they did on the original single. The original version found on the "Three" EP has not been issued on CD.

"Out of Control" has been a staple of live shows over the years, and still gets featured occasionally. During performances Bono will often spray water into the crowd, an act that many fans refer to as being "Bonotized."

"Stories for Boys"
Lyrics/Music: U2
Producer: Lillywhite

"Stories for Boys" had also appeared on U2's "Three" EP. Like "Out of Control" the song was rerecorded for *Boy* with Lillywhite.

Bono described the song:

> I can remember as a child, looking in the mirror and thinking, "I don't look like that!" That's wrong. You're bombarded with all these images in the comics and nobody's like that. But the effect is of total disillusionment with yourself. You put on a mask and hide from yourself, from your own soul, from what you've got to offer. It's a reaction away from the individual and we stand for individualism.[8]

On more recent recordings such as *The Complete U2*, the 2008 reissue of *Boy* and the fortieth anniversary reissue of "Three," it is not the original version from the "Three" EP but rather an alternate recording which had appeared on the *Just for Kicks* album. The album was a compilation of songs from up-and-coming Dublin bands and featured a demo version of the song. The compilation also featured Edge playing with another Dublin band The Teen Commandments.

The song was covered by Martha Wainwright working with The Separate in 2010.

"The Ocean"
Lyrics/Music: U2
Producer: Lillywhite

"The Ocean" is a song short on lyrics, but big on emotions. Bono shared:

> ... it is the thought of every teenager, it is the thought of everybody in a band who thinks he can change the world. There is another verse which got left out, it's on the sleeve, "When I looked around/The world couldn't be found/Just me by the sea,"

which is the resignation that no matter what you do, people are going to go their own way.[9]

Dorian Gray, named in the lyric, comes from *The Picture of Dorian Gray*, a novel by Oscar Wilde. Gray sells his soul so that his portrait ages instead of himself. The portrait becomes a record of all his sins.

In 2018, Bono would introduce the song while an ocean of blue lights flickered on screen:

Tonight, is a very personal story. The boy's search for his manhood. The boy struggles to hold onto his innocence. He fails. Only later to discover, at the far end of experience, with some wisdom and good company, he can yet again recover that innocence. It's also a story about a boy's search for his mother. The recovery of memories, memories lost in a household that never mentioned her name, after she was lost to us. Her name was Iris. She was my mother.[10]

The song was not performed between 1982 and its reappearance on the Vertigo Tour in 2005.

"A DAY WITHOUT ME"
Lyrics/Music: U2
Producer: Lillywhite

"A Day Without Me" was the first song U2 recorded with producer Steve Lillywhite. It was released as a single two months before the album. Although sometimes identified as being about the suicide of Joy Division lead singer Ian Curtis, the song had been played in full long before the death of Curtis. Bono, however, did confirm it is about suicide, "Our emotions aren't just glossy, throwaway things. Some people saw 'A Day Without Me' as escapism, but it was about suicide."[11] Early press releases from Island Records did state that the song was "based, loosely, on the death of Ian Curtis. U2 were deeply affected by his death as they felt that it was a senseless waste of human life."[12]

Ahead of going into the studio with Lillywhite, U2 worked on the song in session at RTÉ Radio wanting to impress Lillywhite, ensuring he'd stay to do the album. Lillywhite remembered in 2020:

We agreed to do a single first, which was "A Day Without Me," which I didn't think sounded very good. I wanted to change the way that we recorded the band for the rest of the album, and it's quite well known that I decided to put Larry out in the hallway, where the receptionist sat in Windmill Lane, because the drum sound was just not very good on "A Day Without Me," but the drums we recorded for the album were much more exciting.[13]

The album version of "A Day Without Me" was the first single released from *Boy*. The cover is the Booterstown railway station in silver and black. The single was U2's first release outside of UK and Ireland, as Island started testing the band in new regions including the Netherlands, Germany, and France. The song also played a role in breaking U2 in the USA. DJ Carter Alan had found the single as an import and started playing it on his show on WBCN Radio, bringing U2 some early buzz.

The song has not been played in full since 1985, although Bono does occasionally sing a bit of the lyrics in other songs. The single was named the #2 best single for 1980 in the *Hot Press Magazine* Awards in January 1981 ("11 O'Clock Tick Tock" took first place).

"ANOTHER TIME, ANOTHER PLACE"
Lyrics/Music: U2
Producer: Lillywhite

"Another Time, Another Place" may discuss a young teenage couple trying to find their own private space, or perhaps it is just Bono waking up alone and wishing someone were with him. U2 had recorded the song prior to the *Boy* sessions. A demo was recorded at Eamon Andrews studio in February 1979, but the song was rerecorded with Steve Lillywhite for *Boy*.

The song shares its name with a fan club album released in 2015, of a performance at The Marquee Club in London. The song does not appear on the album but in a spoken word piece at the end of that album, Bono does discuss the songs from that time, "But the ideas are sublime. In a rock'n'roll that was obsessed by the defacement and deflowering of innocence we were celebrating the holding on to it."[14]

The song appears to be in retirement currently, not played at a U2 show since 1982.

"THE ELECTRIC CO."
Lyrics/Music: U2
Producer: Lillywhite

"The Electric Co." refers to electroconvulsive therapy (ECT). The song was written about a friend of Bono's taken to a Dublin psychiatric facility, where these shock treatments were in use as medical treatment.

Looking back at *Boy* in 2020, Adam Clayton singled out the song:

> The Electric Co, one of my favourites from our debut album, *Boy*. When we used to play it back then, there's this breakdown in the middle, where Bono would disappear off and we'd be looking around. Edge and I would be checking each other and saying, "where's he gone? where's he gone?" Usually, we'd find him halfway up a piece of scaffolding, waving a flag, or smoking a cigarette, or just interacting with whoever he could find. And then we'd wait until he came back to the stage and then power into the outro, it's always been fun, it's always been fast.[15]

The song is often accompanied live in concerts by short passages of "Send in the Clowns" from the musical *A Little Night Music*. U2 included this snippet on *Under a Blood Red Sky*. They did not get permission however, and faced legal action, finally agreeing to settle with the songwriter for $50,000 and an agreement that the song would be removed from all future pressings of this or any other album.

"Shadows and Tall Trees"
Lyrics/Music: U2
Producer: Lillywhite

"Shadows and Tall Trees" is named from the seventh chapter of William Golding's novel *Lord of the Flies*. In that chapter, the group of boys tackle their fear of the dark and animals hiding within. In his youth, Bono had his own group of boys that called themselves Lypton Village. They would hang out and try to escape their surroundings by escaping into their imaginations. Bono's closest friends, Gavin Friday and Guggi, were part of the group with him, and their new names originated from the group.

The song itself was an early demo recorded with Barry Devlin in November 1978. The entire demo was released in 2004 as part of *The Complete U2* on iTunes. The song was rerecorded with Lillywhite for *Boy*.

It is surprising perhaps that the song was rerecorded for *Boy*. It was rarely played, even in the early days, and there is no knowledge of any performances of the song after mid-1980. By the time U2 were working on the album, it appears that the song had already been abandoned. In one review of U2's performances in McGonagles in 1979 it is oddly called "The Ghost of Shadows of Princess and Tall Trees."

"SATURDAY MATINEE"

Lyrics/Music: U2
Producer: Lillywhite

Early copies of *Boy* on vinyl included a thirty-second instrumental at the end. This were left off in many regions and not included on cassette or CD. The brief instrumental piece was an early version of "Fire," a song that would be developed further with Lillywhite and released on *October*. It was mastered so it is low in volume compared to the rest of the album.

In 2008, the thirty-second instrumental was returned to the end of the album on all pressings. Thanks to digital services, fans learned it had a name, "Saturday Matinee." A longer version of the song, a demo called "Saturday Night" was released on deluxe versions of the album.

Extras from the Era

"The Fool" and "Street Missions" were recorded with Barry Devlin in November 1978, along with "Shadows and Tall Trees." The entire demo was released as part of *The Complete U2* on iTunes.

"Boy/Girl" was one of the three tracks on U2's first EP "Three" and a live version was later released on the B-side to "I Will Follow." It was another early track which featured Bono playing with early relationships in the lyrics.

"Another Day" was U2's second single (Ireland only). The song was recorded after U2 finished their first UK tour, and Bono's voice is rough in the mix. The release was timed to coincide with a concert at Dublin Stadium that was broadcast on RTÉ2 radio. After that very concert, U2 signed their contract with Island Records. Another song, "Cartoon World" from that concert appears on the deluxe version of *Boy* in 2008, but no studio version has ever been released.

"11 O'Clock Tick Tock" was U2's first single outside of Ireland, and third single overall. It started life as a song called "Silver Lining" and was recorded with Martin Hannett for their Island Records debut. The single was backed with "Touch," another song which would not appear on the album.

"Speed of Life" was a track recorded with Steve Lillywhite for *Boy* which never progressed to lyrics. The version released is instrumental and was first released in 2008 on deluxe editions of *Boy*. "Things to Make and Do" was another instrumental B-side that featured on the "A Day Without Me" single.

2
October
(1981)

October was recorded with Steve Lillywhite between July and September 1981. The band finished touring in early June and spent three weeks rehearsing at their old school Mount Temple before entering the recording studio at Windmill Lane. The album was released on October 12, 1981.

Bono, The Edge, and Larry Mullen had joined a religious group, the Shalom Fellowship, which led them to questioning if they should be in a rock band. Adam Clayton was feeling more and more isolated, and the band was struggling. During the tour in the US, Bono had lost his briefcase holding all his notes and ideas for the new album, causing him to start again developing songs in rehearsal. Bono said, "there's a sort of peace about the album, even though it was recorded under that pressure."[1] Being short on material for the album, U2 also included the song "Fire," recorded in the Bahamas, earlier released as a single.

The cover design was by Steve Averill, featuring a photograph of U2 at the Grand Canal Docks in Dublin. This area was near Windmill Lane and is steps away where U2 would eventually set up their own studio at Hanover Quay.

The album reached #11 in the UK Charts and #104 in the Hot 200 Chart in the USA.

In 2008, the album was remastered under direction by The Edge and released with an additional disc containing related studio material, and live performances from the era.

"GLORIA"
Lyrics/Music: U2
Producer: Lillywhite

"Gloria" may appear to be a love song, but the lyrics in Latin translate to "Glory to you, Lord." While recording *October*, Edge, Bono, and Larry Mullen had joined an organization called Shalom and were exploring religion deeply. Bono explained:

Gloria, people have talked about it being a name. In fact, it's a piece of Latin.... That may sound pretentious. But that's what it is. I'd been listening to some mass type music, a sort of choral type music. I'm very interested in choral music, cathedral type music. Gloria is also obviously a name of a person or a girl. It can be a love song, but it's more than that.[2]

"Gloria" was listed among song names in Bono's notebook lost on tour. In *Race of Angels* Bono said the song "still makes me smile. It's so wonderfully mad and epic and operatic."[3]

"Gloria" was released as the second single from *October* and the cover used mirrors to make a variation on the album cover (in the Netherlands and New Zealand different covers were used). Several edits appeared ranging from twenty seconds removed (UK promo single) to almost two full minutes removed (Argentina promo single). In the UK the single reached #55 in the UK Charts.

U2 filmed a music video for "Gloria" with Meiert Avis featuring U2 in the Grand Canal docks area. U2 appear on a barge while a crowd gathers to cheer them on. In America, the video landed as MTV launched (August 1, 1981) and was placed in heavy rotation as there was a shortage of video clips to play on air.

In 2021 U2 issued a fortieth anniversary edition of "Gloria." To celebrate the song's reoccurring spot in setlists over the years, the yellow 12-inch features a live version from 1990 (minutes after the year had started), from the 2000s and the 2010s.

Huey Morgan, lead singer of the Fun Lovin' Criminals has identified "Gloria" as one of his favourite U2 songs.

"I Fall Down"
Lyrics/Music: U2
Producer: Lillywhite

U2 was not totally unprepared to record "I Fall Down," which was developed during early 1981 tour dates in North America. The song debuted in Cincinnati, regularly performed prior to the album sessions. The song was also mentioned in several places in Bono's lost notebook.

Who was Julie, mentioned in the song? In *Into the Heart* both Bono and Gavin Friday discuss Julie, a girl Bono brought on stage during the March 1981 shows in New York. She ended up getting involved with a member of U2's crew and moving to Ireland. Even Bono seems unsure if she inspired the lyric.

The song often appeared in live sets in early shows but has only been played once since 1985. Long-time U2 set designer Willie Williams has named "I Fall Down" as one of his favourite U2 songs.

"I Threw a Brick Through a Window"
Lyrics/Music: U2
Producer: Lillywhite

"I Threw a Brick Through a Window" is described by Bono as being "about not liking yourself. It's seeing your reflection in the window and wanting to smash it."[4] U2 had spent months on the road, returning home to record a second album. They were struggling. Bono would share:

> Most of the lyrics were written on the microphone. At £50 an hour that creates quite a pressure because Steve Lillywhite is sitting there and he's waiting for me and I'm not going to sing anything I don't feel right about. So, I would sing the songs under this pressure trying to get across what was going on in my life.[5]

Like "I Fall Down," the song was popular in early shows but was only played twice since 1984.

"Rejoice"
Lyrics/Music: U2
Producer: Lillywhite

"Rejoice" was newly created in studio with the music being developed during practice sessions at Mount Temple ahead of entering Windmill. The lyrics were made up during recording, with Bono leaning on some of the spiritual ideas he was discussing when meeting with the Shalom group. The song was played throughout 1982 as part of the October tour stops, but it has not been played since.

It would have been a mostly forgotten song until "Lucifer's Hands" was released in 2014. Bono mentioned the connection in 2017:

> The core of "Innocence" to me is a lyric from our second album, which says, "I can't change the world, but I can change the world in me." The core of "Experience" is—and this is cheeky!—"I can change the world, but I can't change the world in me." And so, you realize that the biggest obstacle in the way is yourself. There are things to rail against, and there are things that deserve your rage, and you must plot and conspire to overthrow them. But the most wily and fearsome of your enemies is going to turn out to be yourself. And that's experience.[6]

Even the most neglected songs can become fodder for later ideas.

"Fire"
Lyrics/Music: U2
Producer: Lillywhite

"Fire" grew out of a short instrumental piece that U2 had worked on in the last days of recording *Boy* and had included thirty seconds of at the end of the album. The song would be recorded as a demo called "Saturday Night" and was later reworked into "Fire." The Edge discussing "Saturday Night" says "Listening back now I can't help feeling that we lost some of the power and directness of the original."[7]

"Fire" was the one song on the album not recorded at Windmill Lane. Although started in Dublin, the song was finished at Compass Point Studios, in Nassau, Bahamas, a studio founded by Chris Blackwell, president of Island Records. Steve Lillywhite had joined the band on their US tour, and the five took a working vacation to Nassau between US tour dates to record.

"Fire" debuted live in concert in New Haven, CT, two months before it was released as a single, months before *October*. "Fire" reached #35 on the UK Charts, and earned U2 an invitation to appear on *Top of the Pops*, a popular UK program. There was disappointment from some in the U2 camp that the song had not done better. Lillywhite shared, "Yeah, that was a little bit of a letdown. And I don't think it was one of the greatest U2 songs. Although it's probably a bit better than 'A Celebration', right?"[8] Larry Mullen had a different take when asked about the lack of chart success with the single. "We release what we want to release. Chart success isn't important. Just getting up on stage every night, the live appearance, that's what's important to me."[9]

In Germany, the Netherlands, and Spain, the release was a 12-inch format, with a unique sleeve, titled "U2 R.O.K." The "R.O.K." version of the single is also the earliest single available on CD, via a 1991 pressing in Austria. The original single had a black sleeve with an image of the sun on the front cover. The "R.O.K." versions had a yellow cover with Bono in black and white.

In 2021 for the fortieth anniversary of the single, U2 issued a 12-inch picture disc of the song for Record Store Day, with artwork showing a blazing ring of fire on a black background. The single includes two live versions of "Fire" recorded in 1982 as well as the original B-side.

"Tomorrow"
Lyrics/Music: U2
Producer: Lillywhite

For "Tomorrow" U2 embraced traditional Irish music. They recruited Vincent Kilduff to play the uillean pipes on this song. Kilduff, known for his later work with the Waterboys, was introduced to U2 by tour manager Steve Iredale. Kilduff not only joined U2 on the album, but he also joined U2 for a few shows to celebrate the album, including the live debut of many *October* songs at an appearance at Slane Castle.

Bono spoke about the use of the pipes on the track:

> I've tried in an emotional way to talk about my country. Using the uilleann pipes I'm making a point that it is at home I'm talking about. It shocked me when I realized how little I was aware of the struggle in Northern Ireland, 50 miles up the road from where I walk my dog, where soldiers in Ireland, in Northern Ireland, who themselves probably don't want to be there. It's all a very sad situation, of which I have no wish to make and decisions on in any way, so I tried to look at it in an emotional way. The song is written from a mother's point of view to her son, wondering "will you be back tomorrow."[10]

In later years Bono would realize the song was not just about the Troubles in Northern Ireland. He was subconsciously writing about his own mother's funeral, with many images lifted from his own memories of that day.

In 1996, an album celebrating the work of Donal Lunny was released, *Common Ground*. Lunny is an Irish folk musician and played on each track with the artists featured. Adam and Bono recorded a new version of "Tomorrow" with Lunny. The remake takes the Irish elements of the original, and brings them to the forefront, with accompaniment by accordion, bouzouki, and bodhran.

"OCTOBER"
Lyrics/Music: U2
Producer: Lillywhite

"October" is a slow, haunted piece featuring The Edge on piano. Bono's lyrics reach for the spiritual again. Edge remembers working on the song in *U2 by U2*:

> I really don't know where that "October" piece came from, other than just sitting at a piano and that's where it brought me, into this quite stark, quite grey but beautiful European place. After going on tour through Europe, seeing Paris, Amsterdam, Berlin, and Hamburg in winter, I never felt so European.[11]

Bono confirms that the album title came first, and the song came later, and the name is mentioned in the pages of Bono's missing notebook.

Although never released as a single, "October" received additional exposure when it featured on the soundtrack, *They Call it An Accident*. The French film released in 1982 featured a soundtrack by Steve Winwood, Marianne Faithfull, and other Island Records artists. "October" features on the soundtrack twice, once an instrumental edit of the song, and the other a remix of the song by Wally Badarou.

In 2015, U2 revisited the song on tour accompanying the song with visuals of bombed-out buildings and streets that had been destroyed in the Syrian war leading to a refugee crisis in Europe. The song and visuals combined to make a show stopping moment.

Supermodel Helena Christensen has named "October" as one of her favourite U2 songs.

"WITH A SHOUT"
Lyrics/Music: U2
Producer: Lillywhite

Although known as "With a Shout" in North America, in many other countries the song was labeled "With a Shout (Jerusalem)." The lyrics of the song recall the crucifixion of Christ. The song features an uncredited trumpet. Although identified in some resources as being played from someone in the band Some Kind of Wonderful, I spoke with Paul Bibby, the drummer for the band, and he denies any involvement from any of their members in the album.

"STRANGER IN A STRANGE LAND"
Lyrics/Music: U2
Producer: Lillywhite

Adam Clayton in a 2021 interview on U2 X-Radio explained "Stranger in a Strange Land" was about feeling lost while being away from home on endless tours. He explained the lyrics recalled scenes in Germany while touring the *Boy* album.

Bono told the BBC:

It was inspired by a trip through East Germany, through the border. The border, the terminal that goes from West Germany through East Germany into Berlin, where we met some soldiers. One of them was about my own age. He looked at me, to watch out, that I wasn't going to run, when I felt that maybe he should have been running.[12]

Bono was asked if the song had any ties to the Robert Heinlein novel of the same name, which had inspired a Bowie song. "None at all. It's a song about alienation, I think that novel is a sort of science fiction novel. If there's any connection with the word alien that's all."[13]

"Stranger in A Strange Land" has never been performed live in concert in full to our knowledge and has only been performed as part of another song once.

"Scarlet"
Lyrics/Music: U2
Producer: Lillywhite

The album suffered from a time crunch. A five-week studio booking had stretched into six. U2 had to put the finishes on the album and Bono was still working on lyrics. "Scarlet" has one lyric, Bono singing the word "Rejoice" multiple times (yet it is another song on the album that is called "Rejoice").

Bono explained, "A lot of people found *October* hard to accept at first. I mean, I used the word 'rejoice' precisely because I knew people have a mental block against it. It's a powerful word, it's lovely to say. It's implying more than 'get up and dance, baby'."[14]

"Scarlet" was only played once live in the 1980s in studio at the BBC. But twenty-nine years after the album was released, "Scarlet" was finally performed nightly during the last months of the U2360° Tour.

"Is That All?"
Lyrics/Music: U2
Producer: Lillywhite

"Is That All?" takes a mostly-instrumental song U2 had played for years, "The Cry" and adds vocals. "The Cry" usually was the introduction when U2 played "The Electric Co.." It is first identified as having been played after the release of the *Boy* album, in Edinburgh Scotland on November 21, 1980. Although reworked into "Is That All?" it has never been played in concert, but U2 still include "The Cry" at the start of "The Electric Co.," last heard in 2005 in Montreal. "The Cry" can also be heard at the start of "The Electric Co." on *Under a Blood Red Sky*, U2's 1983 live album. In *U2 by U2* Larry comments, "The album turned out a lot better than I thought it would. I felt the songs were good, we just didn't know how to finish them."[15]

Extras from the Era

"J. Swallow" is called "Johnny Swallow" or "J. Swallo" on some releases. U2 needed a B-side for the "Fire" single and took the drums from another song, slowed them down, building a new song overtop. The song gives us few clues as to who Johnny might have been, but it may have been a reference to one of the nicknames given out by Lypton Village.

"A Celebration" was a single produced by Lillywhite, released between *October* and *War* and recorded as U2 were coming off tour. A video for the song filmed by

Meiert Avis has U2 performing in Dublin's Kilmainham Gaol mixed with footage of an apocalyptic landscape. The song deals with the atomic bomb and trying to celebrate in the face of pending war. It charted at #47 on the UK Charts. The B-side was "Trash, Trampoline and the Party Girl" a celebratory song, which thanks to its appearance on the *Under a Blood Red Sky* live album as "Party Girl" is far better known.

A fortieth anniversary edition of "A Celebration" was announced for Record Store Day in 2022. It includes the original tracks, as well as a demo version of "A Celebration" and a live version of "Party Girl" from 2015, taken from a night when a young fan joined the band on guitar in Germany.

3

War
(1983)

War was released on February 28, 1983. The band contemplated alternate producers for the album, even considering a different producer for every track, but in the end, they worked with Steve Lillywhite, on all but one track. Other producers considered included Sandy Pearlman, Jimmy Destri of Blondie, and Bill Whelan. Recording started in August 1982 and continued through October. U2 found themselves running out of studio time at the end, and the last songs recorded as they were being thrown out of the studio.

The album designs are by Steve Averill. U2 once again featured Peter Rowen (sporting a split lip) on the cover, photographed in a similar pose to the photo used for *Boy*. The band wanted a different vision of war than expected images of tanks and guns.

War was U2's first #1 in the UK, knocking Michael Jackson's *Thriller* off the top spot. In the US U2 reached #12 with "War." The album was given the award for Best Sleeve and Best Album in the 1983 *Hot Press* Awards. It is listed in Robert Dimery's *1001 Albums You Must Hear Before You Die*, and *Rolling Stone* included it in their Top 500 Albums at #221 in the 2003 list and #223 in the 2012 list.

In 1993, a remastered version of *War* was released by Mobile Fidelity. The company went back to the original master tapes resulting in differences from the regular commercial release of *War* including longer songs. These are unique to the Mobile Fidelity release. In 2008, a remastered version of the album directed by The Edge was released with an additional disc of studio and live tracks from the *War* era, including one song from the original sessions which was newly finished for the release.

"SUNDAY BLOODY SUNDAY"
Lyrics/Music: U2
Producer: Lillywhite

"Sunday Bloody Sunday" deals with the conflicts known as the Troubles in Ireland. Adam explained, "It isn't so much about the Troubles in a physical sense, but about the human carnage of families being wrecked."[1] Bloody Sunday refers to different incidents in the Troubles, most commonly the 1972 incident where British troops shot and killed several unarmed civil rights performers in Derry. That incident inspired John Lennon and Yoko Ono to create their own song titled "Sunday Bloody Sunday." Another incident in Irish history known as Bloody Sunday happened in 1920 during the Irish War of Independence. British forces raided a football match at Croke Park, opening fire on spectators and athletes. Another day sharing the name happened in Belfast the following year when the IRA ambushed police in the city.

The song title was mentioned in the notebook that Bono lost during the preparation of the *October* album. It was not developed further until U2 started to work on *War*. While others in U2 took some time off with Bono heading on his honeymoon, The Edge sat down and fleshed out the lyric of the song. He explains:

> We all had a hand in that song because it's probably the heaviest thing we've ever done, lyrically. It's hard for us to justify a title like "Sunday Bloody Sunday," and we are aware of that. We realize the potential for division in a song like that, so all we can say is that we're trying to confront the subject rather than sweep it under the carpet. We thought a lot about the song before we played it in Belfast and Bono told the audience that if they didn't like it then we'd never play it again. Out of the 3,000 people in the hall about three walked out. I think that says a lot about the audience's trust in us.[2]

In most countries, "Two Hearts Beat as One" was released as the second single. "Sunday Bloody Sunday" was chosen instead for the Netherlands, Germany, Spain, and Brazil. In Japan, both were released. Both "Two Hearts" and "Sunday Bloody Sunday" used the same cover with Peter Rowen, and the same B-side. In Japan, the cover featured images of U2 performing live.

There was no dedicated video for the song, but to promote *Under a Blood Red Sky*, a standalone live performance taken from Red Rocks was distributed for promotion.

U2 have released several live performances of "Sunday Bloody Sunday." Of note is the acoustic performance of the song with The Edge on vocals, taken from U2's appearance in Sarajevo in 1997. It featured on the "If God Will Send His Angels" single. A live performance in 1987 at Croke Park in Dublin appears over the final credits of *Bloody Sunday*, a 2002 film by Paul Greengrass about the shootings in Derry in 1972. To mark the fiftieth anniversary in 2022 of Bloody Sunday, Bono and The Edge shared an acoustic performance of the song on social media.

"Sunday Bloody Sunday" was listed at #18 on the 40 Best Tracks of the 1980s by *Q Magazine* in 2006. *Rolling Stone* placed it on their list of the 500 Greatest

Songs of All Time, coming in at #268 in 2004 and #272 in 2010. The song is one of four U2 songs on a list curated by James Henke of the Rock and Roll Hall of Fame of the 500 Songs That Shaped Rock and Roll. It is the earliest U2 song to feature on that list. The song was U2's fifth most streamed song at the end of 2021 on Spotify.

"Sunday Bloody Sunday" was covered by Saul Williams in 2007, produced and arranged by Trent Reznor of Nine Inch Nails.

"SECONDS"
Lyrics/Music: U2
Producer: Lillywhite

"Seconds" opens with Edge's voice and not Bono's, although Bono can be heard in the mix as well. The Edge discussed the track, "I'm not keen on my voice to be honest. I think that this song is, which hasn't been particularly shown on other tracks on our album, is the tongue in cheek humor which we have as well."[3]

Midway through the song we hear a sample taken from the documentary *Soldier Girls*, which Bono had been watching during the recording of *War*. It is U2's first identified use of a sample:

> It is a serious song but we're not taking it too seriously. It could be called do the atomic bomb, it has references to the nuclear predicament, but it's much more than that. Also, we taped a documentary about the girls in the US army. It was unbelievable to see these girls being wound up…. They are chanting away, kill, kill.[4]

A remaster of *War* by Mobile Fidelity has a ten-second longer version of "Seconds" due to a longer sample from *Soldier Girls*.

The song has not been performed live since The Unforgettable Fire Tour.

"NEW YEAR'S DAY"
Lyrics/Music: U2
Producer: Lillywhite

The lyrics for "New Year's Day" were inspired by the solidarity movement in Poland unfolding as U2 was recording *War*. Solidarity was the trade union founded in 1980 by Lech Wałęsa, with over one third of the working population of Poland as members. The union played an important role in the end of the Communist rule in Poland, and Wałęsa would eventually be elected president. Musically, the song initially developed as Adam Clayton attempted to play Visage's song, "Fade to Grey" during a soundcheck.

The song was released as the first single from *War*, January 10, 1983. An edit of the track featured on the single release (and a different edit in Japan). Remixes of "New Year's Day" by Steve Lillywhite and François Kevorkian were also issued with the single. In the charts, the song reached #10 in the UK, the band's first appearance in the Top 10. The single was U2's first to chart on the *Billboard* Hot 100 in the USA, reaching #53 on the chart.

A video filmed by Meiert Avis in Sweden depicts U2 performing on a snowy landscape, mixed with clips of four riders on horseback in the same setting. Although their faces are covered, they are not U2, these "horsemen" are four teenage girls. The band had frozen during shooting the day before, and enlisted the four teens to stand in. The clip also incorporates archival footage of Soviet troops in winter.

The roots of the song have not been forgotten by fans in Poland. During a 2005 tour stop, local fans held up coloured items during the song. Those on the lower levels held up red, while those higher up waved white items. This formed a large version of the Polish flag which stunned U2 on stage.

Leading up to 2000, U2 approached DJ Ferry Corsten to remix the track with plans to issue the single for the New Year. The Edge explained in the 2008 reissue of *War* that they had left the remix too late to complete, but it was included on the deluxe reissue. In 2018, as Brexit loomed and Europe became a focus of U2's live show, "New Year's Day" was remixed by St Francis Hotel. The remix, and a live recording of U2 performing it on the 2018 tour were both included on "The Europa EP" released for Record Store Day in 2018. The version on the Mobile Fidelity pressing in the late 1990s includes the full measure before Edge's guitar solo which is missing on other versions of *War*.

The song has been named on *Rolling Stone*'s lists of 500 Greatest Songs of All Times, ranking at #427 in 2004 and #435 in 2010. In the *Hot Press* Awards for 1983, it was ranked the #2 best single and best video. "New Year's Day" was kept out of the number one position in the Irish charts by "Down Under" by Men at Work, peaking at #2 in the charts. In 2001, a dance track sampling "New Year's Day" called "New Year's Dub" was credited to Musique vs U2, and reached #15 in the UK charts, and U2 even made an appearance in the video.

The song has been covered by several artists and sampled by many more. One cover saw teen pop idol Tiffany join Canadian electro-industrial band Front Line Assembly to record the song for a tribute album.

"LIKE A SONG..."
Lyrics/Music: U2
Producer: Lillywhite

"Like a Song..." was Bono commenting on the punk movement. It invokes the leather, lace and chains, badges, and uniforms that made up the punk wardrobe.

Bono used it as a message to journalists who were critical of U2 not being punk enough.

It is believed that "Like a Song..." was only played once at the opening show of the 1983 tour, and never performed again. There is certainly no record of another performance.

A longer version of the song is found on the 1990s master of *War* by Mobile Fidelity. Using the original recordings, the master has changes from earlier pressings. In the case of "Like a Song..." the outro of the song is longer.

"DROWNING MAN"
Lyrics/Music: U2
Producer: Lillywhite

The title "Drowning Man" does not appear in the lyrics but comes from a project Bono had worked on with the Royal Dublin Ballet. "It was the title of a Sam Beckett-style play I'd started about a drowning man. I had a few scenes written. There was to be a guy in a chair with a blindfold and there was to be a little ballet thing."[5] During interviews for *War*, Bono and The Edge spoke about working with the choreographer of the Ballet, Arlene Phillips, but the project never came to completion.

Steve Wickham of The Waterboys plays violin on the song and appears on "Sunday Bloody Sunday." The Edge talks about the meeting where Wickham was recruited:

> We were sort of going through a period at home where we were just writing the album. I was getting the bus home one night, which I tend to do when I want some time just to think. I was standing at the bus stop, had one foot on the bus, when this guy ran into me, grabbed me by the arm, and said "I play electric violin, are you looking for a violin player for the album?" I said yeah. We were looking at getting some musicians in.[6]

As with other songs Bono borrows lyrics from the Bible. "But those who wait on the Lord shall renew their strength. They shall mount up with wings like eagles, they shall run and not be weary, they shall walk and not faint" inspires the lyric here and comes from Isaiah 40:31.

The full version of "Drowning Man" has not been performed but lyrics have appeared briefly in other songs. U2 continues to rehearse the song, including rehearsals for 2009's U2360° Tour. In 2009, asked what "one piece of music that really defines U2," Adam Clayton chose "Drowning Man" as his song of choice.[7] The Edge has said "It's one of the most successful pieces of recording we've ever done."[8]

"THE REFUGEE"
Lyrics/Music: U2
Producer: Whelan

"The Refugee" is the only song on *War* not produced by Steve Lillywhite. Bill Whelan, an Irish composer, is the producer here. Whelan was later responsible for *Riverdance*, creating a worldwide interest in Celtic music in the 1990s. Lillywhite mixed the final track, to ensure it fit the album. Leading into *War*, U2 had looked at multiple producers for the album including Whelan, going so far as to record the one song with him.

Bono had taken an interest in the stories of refugees, running from their countries with little in the way of belongings to escape war. For an album titled *War*, Bono spoke about refugees for the first time, but it is a topic that would reappear throughout U2's career.

The song has never been played live in concert.

"TWO HEARTS BEAT AS ONE"
Lyrics/Music: U2
Producer: Lillywhite

Bono got married just before the recording of *War*. His honeymoon was just before work on the album started. The Edge shares, "'Two Hearts' is a love song."[9]

"Two Hearts Beat as One" was the second single released to promote *War*. It was issued worldwide, except for the Netherlands, Germany, Spain, and Brazil, where "Sunday Bloody Sunday" was released instead. "Two Hearts" almost made it to #1 at home in Ireland but was kept out of the top spot by David Bowie's "Let's Dance," peaking at #2 instead. The song did not chart in the US, and it peaked at #18 in the UK Charts.

A video for "Two Hearts Beat as One" was filmed in Montmartre, a hill in the northern part of Paris, France. Directed again by Meiert Avis (his fifth video with U2), it depicts U2 performing on the steps of Sacré-Cœur Basilica. U2 footage is mixed with scenes of Peter Rowen walking around the streets following carnival performers, including an acrobat and a fire-breather.

Two shorter 7-inch edits were done for the single release. The single was accompanied with several remixes of the title track, including remixes by Francois Kervorkian and Steve Lillywhite. U2 had looked at having Kervorkian remix the entire album, but he stopped after two songs, this one and "New Year's Day."

"RED LIGHT"
Lyrics/Music: U2
Producer: Lillywhite

Bono explained, "I certainly remember a fascination with prostitution, we played Amsterdam and I remember seeing the girls for sale in the windows, lit in red. Thinking about it, trying to figure out the reality of it. Whether there was any or not. I was never judgmental about it."

"Red Light" and the next song on the album "Surrender" feature additional guests, trumpet by Kenny Fradley and backing vocals by Cheryl Poirier, Adriana Kaegi, Taryn Hagey of Kid Creole's band, The Coconuts, and Jessica Felton. Lillywhite looking back at the album in 2008 said:

> One of the strange things about that album is that we used Kid Creole's backing singers, the Coconuts. They just happened to be in Dublin on tour, so we hung out with them and they came in and sang on "Surrender." So, it was sort of random—this serious Irish rock band having the Coconuts on their album. But there's nothing U2 like better than a pretty woman.[10]

Bono described the atmosphere while recording, with the studio lit in red, and one of the Coconuts dressing in a revealing outfit. "The boys from Ireland had difficulty breathing," he remembers. [11]

The song has never been performed live.

"SURRENDER"
Lyrics/Music: U2
Producer: Lillywhite

"Surrender" also includes the Coconuts on backing vocals. Although some sources suggest they had been involved on three tracks, Steve Lillywhite confirms that it was indeed only these two songs. "Surrender" is inspired by the city of New York, and a visit to the city. Bono shared:

> It's a lot to do with the friction in the city, the friction that I experienced in New York, a lot of what people call street hustle. I had this picture of the band; they would play at the very top of one of the tall buildings there for a video. And to this, there's a place above it all, a place of surrender. A lot of friction is caused by ego, pride, and I think the idea of dying to yourself ... the last line of the song is if I want to live, I got to die to myself ... which is basically stepping down. Especially in this country, there's been a lot of hassle caused by people who step up. Stand up for what you believe. In fact, that's lead us all into a lot of trouble. I think some passive resistance is needed around here.[12]

"Surrender" has not been performed live since The Unforgettable Fire Tour.

"40"

Lyrics/Music: U2
Producer: Lillywhite

"40" was the final song recorded as U2 were being thrown out of the studio. It was so late in the recording process that Adam Clayton had already left, and the song was recorded without him. Short on time, Bono borrowed lines from Psalm 40, giving the song its name. Bono has claimed "there's a great peace about the song."[13]

Bono said of the song:

> It's a very sensitive atmospheric track. It was written in a half an hour ... we were being thrown out of the studio, people were lying on the ground shattered, everyone probably just wanted to give up. We just stood up, at least I stood up, Edge you were probably still lying down. We walked to the microphone and I sang this song.[14]

The Edge responds:

> One of the aspects of the band is the fact that there are times we can almost do a song instantly. A lot of the melodies to this song were for another piece, it just so happened that something that we'd put together earlier on, fitted together, just clicked, incredible, and in the sort of excitement that followed we just came out with this song. It's a kind of monument to U2 in an instant.[15]

Released as a single in Germany, "40" was the final single from *War*. In August, U2 had performed at the Rockpalast summer festival, a televised show held at Loreley Amphitheatre in Sankt Goarshausen, Germany. The strong performance garnered much attention in the music press, and to capitalize on the situation, a 7-inch single was pressed exclusively for the German market. The sleeve called U2 "The discovery of Loreley '83." The version of "40" used on the single is a very slight edit of the album version.

Live in concert, "40" has closed many shows. During live performances Adam Clayton and The Edge would switch instruments and positions on stage. And as the song ends, U2 leave the stage one-by-one, until Larry Mullen is alone behind the drum kit. Tour manager Dennis Sheehan would go into the crowd encouraging them sing the end refrain over and over, long after Bono had finished. At the first concert after Sheehan's death in 2015, U2 reincorporated the song into their shows and paid tribute to him on screen.

One memorable performance is captured on the fan club release, *From the Ground Up*. Having not played "40" for the entire U2360° Tour, U2 ended the night and the tour with it. Bono opened the song with the Aaronic blessing, and the band gave a beautiful performance to end the tour that had set records for highest-grossing tour and the highest-attended tour of all time.

The Frames, led by Glen Hansard, did a beautiful cover of "40" for a UNICEF Tsunami Relief Fund for the areas ravaged in the Boxing Day tsunami in the Indian Ocean.

Extras from the Era

"Treasure (Whatever Happened to Pete the Chop?)" was the B-side to "New Year's Day." It refers to a song recorded in London in 1979 called "Pete the Chop." U2 worried it was too poppy and decided not to release it. Pete the Chop had been a friend of U2 who requested a song be written for him. The song was re-recorded and rearranged resulting in this B-side. "Endless Deep" was an instrumental that had appeared as a B-side on "Two Hearts Beat as One."

"Angels Too Tied to the Ground" was an unfinished track left over from *War*. In May 2008, U2 went into studio to do additional work on the song, including recording new vocals by Bono. It was released on the 2008 remaster of *War*.

The Unforgettable Fire (1984)

The Unforgettable Fire was released on October 1, 1984 and recorded between May and August 1984. U2 spent a month recording at Slane Castle while U2 and crew lived at the castle. The album was completed at Windmill Studios. U2 worked with producers Brian Eno and Daniel Lanois for the first time.

The covers of the album feature two Irish castles: Moydrum Castle near Athlone on the front and Carriogogunnell Castle near Clarina on the back. The photo on the front on vinyl and CD features the castle and members of U2 off in the distance. The photo on cassette in some regions has the castle at a distance but the full band can be seen in the foreground. The artwork and design of the album was done by long-time collaborator Steve Averill, starting from images taken by Anton Corbijn.

The album debuted at #1 on the UK Albums Chart and reached #12 on the *Billboard* 200 chart in the USA. The album was named #16 by *Hot Press* poll for Greatest Irish Albums of All Time (2005). In the *Hot Press* Awards in 1985, the album took Best Album and Best Album Sleeve.

Accompanying the album, a video titled *The Unforgettable Fire Collection* was released in 1985, a thirty-minute documentary focused on the making of the album, and several videos released for promotion of the album.

The album was remastered by Mobile Fidelity in 1995 going back to the original master recordings resulting in a unique pressing of the album. In 2009 for the album's twenty-fifth anniversary, a new remaster directed by The Edge was released. Included were deluxe versions with an additional disc of bonus material and a boxed set including video from concerts and *The Unforgettable Fire Collection* documentary.

"A SORT OF HOMECOMING"
Lyrics: Bono
Music: U2
Producer: Eno/Lanois

Bono said "A Sort of Homecoming" is "geographical, but I don't know where it's based. When I look at Van Morrison or Bob Dylan, I'm in awe of their tradition, I'm jealous. We haven't got that we aren't plugged into it."[1]

The EP "Wide Awake in America" also features the song, recorded in London in November 1984. It was not live but was rather recorded during a soundcheck, and the crowd noise was added by producer Tony Visconti. An edit of "A Sort of Homecoming" was released as the B-side to "Bad" in South Africa. In 2009, to celebrate the twenty-fifth anniversary of this album, the "Daniel Lanois Mix" of the song was released, featuring additional vocals recorded by Peter Gabriel and Daniel Lanois.

A video, filmed by Barry Devlin, uses the recording from "Wide Awake in America" and was used for promotion of the EP. The video itself features footage taken from multiple stops throughout the 1984 European Tour, including Paris, Brussels, Rotterdam, London, and Glasgow, mixing footage of the performances, set up at venues, and the cities themselves from a moving vehicle.

The song had not been played since the 1980s, when U2 suddenly introduced it to the first show at Slane Castle in 2001. It made another appearance later in that tour when Bono pulled a fan from the audience to play with them, and the fan started playing the opening notes of the song. Bono went with it figuring out the lyrics as he went along. It would not be performed again until The Joshua Tree Tour in 2017.

Chris Martin of Coldplay has named "A Sort of Homecoming" as one of his favourite U2 songs.

"Pride (In the Name of Love)"
Lyrics: Bono
Music: U2
Producer: Eno/Lanois

"Pride (In the Name of Love)" was released in advance of the album with a single featuring a longer version of "Pride." U2 felt it was the lead single from the start. Edge shares "I think the essence of the song is very simple. That's probably why it makes sense as a 45. The original structure was a lot more complex. It was Eno's influence I think that lead us to cut it down, to strip it down to the bare essentials of the piece."[2] Backing vocals on the song are credited to Chrissie Hynde of Pretenders who worked with U2 in studio at Windmill Lane on the final recording of the song.

The song is written about Martin Luther King, Jr. King was a civil rights leader in the US in the 1960s. He was assassinated in 1968. Bono explains:

> I originally wrote "Pride" about Ronald Reagan and the ambivalent attitude in America. It was originally meant as the sort of pride that won't back down, that wants to build nuclear arsenals. But that wasn't working. I remembered a wise old man who said to me, "Don't try and fight darkness with light, just make the light shine brighter." I

was giving Reagan too much importance; then I thought, "Martin Luther King, there's a man." We build the positive rather than fighting with the finger.[3]

There is a historical inaccuracy in the lyrics on the song. Bono sings that King's assassination happened in the early morning, though it actually happened in the evening. Bono is aware of the error and often changes it in concert. In 2012, U2 worked with Tiësto on a new version of the song, and Bono rerecorded the vocal allowing him to correct the error. The remix was released on the digital only *Dance (RED), Save Lives*.

A video directed by Donald Cammell features footage of U2 performing at St Francis Xavier Hall in Dublin, shots around the Dublin Docklands, and the Poolbeg power generating station. A video by Barry Devlin features U2 recording the song filmed at Slane Castle. A third video directed by Anton Corbijn features U2's faces in and out of focus against a grey background. It was Corbijn's first video for U2 and was not widely released.

The song became U2's first Top 40 single on *Billboard*'s Hot 100 chart in the USA, reaching #33. The song reached #3 in the UK charts. In Ireland, "Pride" was the third single in a row which just missed the #1 spot, charting at #2, kept out of the top spot by Stevie Wonder's "I Just Called to Say I Love You."

The song appears at #46 on the *Rolling Stone*'s 100 Best Singles of the Last 25 Years (July 1989). It appears at #378 on the 500 Greatest Songs of All Time in 2004 and #388 on the same list in 2010 by *Rolling Stone*. The song is #65 on *Spin Magazine*'s 100 Greatest Singles of All Time. The song was U2's sixth most streamed song at the end of 2021 on Spotify.

"Pride" was remixed by Karsh Kale and titled the "100 Voices Mix" on "The Eternal EP," an EP of remixes by Indian artists done to celebrate U2's first visit to India in 2019.

"Pride" has been frequently covered by other artists including country artist Dierks Bentley and C+C Music Factory. A cover by Garbage released in 2021 was taken from a performance honouring Bono at the MusiCares award in 2003.

"WIRE"
Lyrics: Bono
Music: U2
Producer: Eno/Lanois

"Wire" developed while Bono was at the microphone. He told Dave Fanning that while he was singing, he was basing his lyrics around an image that he had in his head, "just an image I had of the hypodermic needle. I'm sure it means different things to different people."[4] The song is one of two that touches on the drug epidemic that was gripping Dublin, and Bono had friends who had nearly lost their lives to heroin. "It informs the LP a lot more than people realize. It had a great effect on me. When your friend becomes a junkie, he ceases to be your friend; he'll steal from you, he'll fight you."[5]

The song was considered for a single and U2 approached Francois Kervorkian to remix "Wire" for them. In the end, the remixes were not used by U2 at the time, but the "Celtic Dub Mix" was provided to *NME* to use on a 7-Inch single, given away with their magazine. And for the twenty-fifth anniversary of *The Unforgettable Fire* the "Kervorkian 12″ Vocal Remix" was also released.

In 1999, Jeep Grrlz heavily incorporated U2's "Wire" into their song "Rewired," so much so that many consider it a remix of the U2 song. The Edge had given his blessing to release the single when he heard it, and Island Records approached the act to sign with them. Several remixes of "Rewired" also exist.

"The Unforgettable Fire"
Lyrics: Bono
Music: U2
Producer: Eno/Lanois

"The Unforgettable Fire" title comes from a series of paintings and writings done by survivors of the Hiroshima and Nagasaki atom bombs in Japan. Bono has said that the title goes beyond that and includes the "unforgettable fire" he has seen in people like Martin Luther King, Ghandi, and Elvis Presley. A third meaning behind the title is the unforgettable fire that a drug like heroin or alcohol can have. Adam Clayton said, "I think there's a more sinister connotation with the fire of alcohol and heroin as well. I think it covers all those three areas. There are clues all the way through the album as to which category each song falls into as well."[6]

The lyrics were written while Bono was in Tokyo:

I wrote it in a hotel room [in Tokyo]. People expect U2 to be so up. Sometimes it's confining. Like anyone else sometimes we go down. That particular song documents a lower side. It's very personal. I don't really want to get into it. But I think what people relate to is the mood of the music as well as the words. They were stained on my memory. Being in Tokyo, Tokyo that night looked like a Christmas tree. As an industrial city there are just roads everywhere. There are neon signs everywhere. It lights up like a Christmas tree. I wrote that song which combines so many things from my own feelings.[7]

"The Unforgettable Fire" was the second single from the album but was not released in the United States where the EP "Wide Awake in America" was issued instead. "The Unforgettable Fire" was the first single U2 released that reached #1 in the Irish Charts. The previous three singles had all peaked at #2. In the UK the song reached #5.

The video was filmed by Meiert Avis in Sweden using photographic techniques to film light trails of objects in motion, including traffic and amusement park rides. Other footage includes U2 in the snow, Larry and Adam in an industrial building, and Bono and Larry performing in a darkened room. The images capture Bono's memories of Tokyo, even if they did not film there, the city footage is stock footage from Minneapolis.

The Edge while doing promotion for the album named "The Unforgettable Fire" his favourite of the tracks on the new release.[8]

"PROMENADE"

Lyrics: Bono
Music: U2
Producer: Eno/Lanois

"Promenade" was composed by Bono at the microphone. It has drawn comparisons to Van Morrison and Bono shares, "The song was written in one take. I went to the microphone with a piece of music and just sang it. In some ways it's complete coincidence. The 'radio' image just came to me—and obviously I turned it into that Van lick."[9]

The song's lyrics talk about watching fireworks exploding over a seaside town. Bono was living overlooking Killiney Bay in Bray, complete with spiral staircase, overlooking the water.

Only one version of the song exists, and the song has never been performed live.

"4TH OF JULY"

Lyrics: Bono
Music: U2
Producer: Eno/Lanois

"4th of July" was The Edge and Adam Clayton jamming, and they had no idea the song was being recorded. The Edge shares:

> Myself and Adam were just in one of the rooms in Slane Castle where we recorded the backing tracks, just messing around. Brian had some treatments set up for a vocal effect and he patched the guitar into them. Got a rough mix going, it sounded good, so he just put on the quarter inch tape machine. So "4th of July" never went to 24-track, it just went straight onto stereo tape. So, we've just taken a section of improvised live work, almost, and it just captured a lovely mood.[10]

"4th of July" is another song that has not been performed live. The instrumental was used over the PA prior to U2 taking the stage in concert.

While working on *The Unforgettable Fire*, The Edge became the first member of U2 to become a father with the birth of his daughter Hollie. She was born on the 4th of July, and the song title marks her birth.

Perhaps an interesting coincidence, the castle on the cover of the album, Moydrum Castle, was attacked by the IRA in 1921, and set fire overnight, in the early hours of July 4, leading to the ruin it is in today.

"BAD"

Lyrics: Bono
Music: U2
Producer: Eno/Lanois

The lyrics for "Bad" address the heroin crisis in Dublin, but it is not just about heroin, Bono said, "I said I wrote it for a friend of mine and I also wrote it for myself. Because you can be addicted to anything. That song is not just about heroin. It's about a lot of things. None of our songs really are just about one thing. A whole life has gone into them."[11] "Bad" was born in studio on the microphone like many other songs on the album. Bono was sketching out lyrics as he sang, and "Bad" became about addiction, even though it had not originally been planned that way. The song title came easy to U2, with The Edge revealing:

> It seemed quite an obvious one. In fact, so obvious we questioned it initially. One of the early inspirations for that song was a certain repetitive quality that the Velvet Underground would have used in their earlier days. The song, lyrically, I think seemed to be dedicated to a friend of Bono's who was going through a very bad time with heroin. That title suggested itself quite early in the making of the song. It was one of those working titles we were not sure on. When it came to the end of the record, we had to make a decision. I think everyone was convinced that that was the title really and nothing else could sum it up so well.[12]

"Bad" was one of three songs U2 planned for the Live Aid concert in 1985. U2 opened with "Sunday Bloody Sunday" and then launched into "Bad." During the performance Bono left the stage to pull a girl from the audience while the band played an extended version of "Bad" leaving them insufficient time to perform their third song. Bono thought he had screwed up, but it became one of the most talked about moments of the concert. The performance at Live Aid has been released in video and audio formats.

"Bad" was edited for a single, released only in South Africa. A different edit appears on *The Best of 1980–1990*. A live performance in Birmingham was released on the "Wide Awake in America" EP. This performance is often named as a favourite of many U2 fans, and the title of the EP comes from the lyrics of "Bad." About the song in concert, Bono says:

The idea was about a friend of mine who was strung out very badly on smack. The song was made up on the spot. Unfortunately, we never went over it, because it was felt the recording was a moment and should be left that way. I don't think I've ever sung the exact lyric that is on the record. I play with it every night, which is something I like.[13]

Several other live performances over the years have been released in audio and video formats, and the song continues to be a favourite of U2 to perform live.

"INDIAN SUMMER SKY"
Lyrics: Bono
Music: U2
Producer: Eno/Lanois

"Indian Summer Sky" was written by Bono in advance of going into the studio. Bono shares, "'Indian Summer Sky' was actually written in New York City and it had a sense of wanting to break through a city to an open place. Most of it was cinematic and very fast."[14] The song also was inspired from a conversation that Bono had with a friend about the city of Toronto, and the massacres that had taken place of Native American people. Bono shared his friend, "felt in some way as if there were troubled spirits still there. What I was trying to get across was a sense of a spirit trapped in a concrete jungle—something like that."[15]

The song was only played nine times during The Unforgettable Fire Tour, and only one version of the song has ever been released.

"ELVIS PRESLEY AND AMERICA"
Lyrics: Bono
Music: U2
Producer: Eno/Lanois

Many songs on the album were developed with Bono coming up with lyrics on the spot at the microphone but it is most apparent on "Elvis Presley and America." He is making up some of the words as he goes along, and the lyrics always lead to the question of what Bono is saying.

Bono shares that the song:

Was recorded in five minutes. Eno just handed me a microphone and told me to sing over this piece of music that had been slowed down, played backwards, whatever. I said, 'What, just like that, now?' He said, 'Yes, this is what you're about.' So, I did it and when it was finished there was all these beautiful lines and melodies coming out of it. I said, 'I can't wait to finish this.' He said, 'What do you mean "finish it"? It is finished.[16]

Bono did have Elvis in mind when he was putting words together:

> It was partly a reaction to the Albert Goldman book which tried to portray him as the archetypal rock'n'roll idiot, but the way he held the mike, the way he sang into the mike—this was a genius. But his decline just tore at me and when I picked up the mike, it was a completely off the wall thing and I just began to sing.[17]

Bono would take on Goldman again in 1988 on "God Part II" on the album *Rattle and Hum*. "Elvis Presley and America" has never been performed live.

"MLK"
Lyrics: Bono
Music: U2
Producer: Eno/Lanois

"MLK" continues the tradition of U2 closing an album on a quieter note. Bono returns to Martin Luther King Jr. for inspiration, and the song is named for him. This song calls for MLK to sleep peacefully and wishes that King's dreams come true.

In January 2004, Bono was honoured at the annual Salute to Greatness Awards at the Martin Luther King Center in Atlanta, founded by King's widow, Coretta Scott King. The award celebrated Bono's work with HIV/AIDS, and his work with debt cancellation in Africa. At the awards ceremony he discussed "MLK" as "a sort of a lullaby for an idea that was dying in our country: the idea of non-violence.... All inspired by a black reverend from Atlanta who refused to hate because he thought love would do a better job."[18]

One special live performance at the 2002 Super Bowl halftime show marked the loss of life during the September 11 attacks. Behind U2 scrolled the names of the victims, firefighters, and others first responders who lost their lives that day as "MLK" was performed. The scrolling of names continued into the next song, "Where the Streets Have No Name." It was a beautiful, touching moment in the middle of one of the biggest events of the year.

Extras from the Era

"Boomerang" was a B-side to "Pride" and two versions were issued, I and II. Both include similar backing music, with the first being mostly an instrumental track, and the second longer version including vocals. "Bass Trap" and "Sixty Seconds in Kingdom Come" were two additional instrumentals released on the single "The Unforgettable Fire." Another instrumental, "Yoshino Blossom" was issued for the twenty-fifth anniversary set.

"Love Comes Tumbling" and "The Three Sunrises" are two songs which appeared both on the "Wide Awake in America" EP and "The Unforgettable Fire" single. Both songs were extra tracks from the Slane Castle recording sessions. The version of "Love Comes Tumbling" varies between the EP and the single with a slightly different intro. In Australia, an alternate vocal mix of "Love Comes Tumbling" was released. The "Wide Awake in America" EP was released in North America on May 20, 1985 and has been kept in print since that time.

5

The Joshua Tree
(1987)

The Joshua Tree was released March 9, 1987. Recording started at Danesmoate House in Rathfarnham; a house Adam Clayton would eventually buy. U2 also recorded at The Edge's house, Melbeach, and at Windmill Lane Studios. Brian Eno and Daniel Lanois returned as producers and Steve Lillywhite returned to offer additional production on the album.

Three covers, using three different photographs of U2, were designed, one for each format released. The cover art for the album has been recognized by *Rolling Stone* as being in the 100 Greatest Album Covers of All Time (#97). Design was by Steve Averill and photography by Anton Corbijn. Both traveled with the band on a road trip through California where the covers were born.

The title refers to a yucca tree which grows in California, the one on the back cover was photographed just outside of Death Valley. That tree fell in 2000, possibly struck by lightning. Visiting the tree has become a pilgrimage for many fans and a plaque near the fallen tree asks, "Have you found what you're looking for?" The photos of the band for the covers were shot at nearby Zabriskie Point.

The album was U2's first album to reach #1 in the USA. It reached #1 in the UK. Record stores opened at midnight to meet demand. Lou Maglia, president of Island Records, shared that the album was "the most complete merchandising effort ever assembled in my career."[1] Island put $100,000 into marketing efforts in the USA alone, producing posters, banners, and instore displays.

U2 won their first Grammy Awards for the album, Album of the Year and Best Rock Performance by a Duo or a Group with Vocal. *The Joshua Tree* was named #6 in *Q Magazine*'s 250 Best Albums of Q's Lifetime (2011), #27 in *Rolling Stone*'s "Top 500 Albums" (2012), and #4 in *Spin*'s "Best Albums of All Time" (1991). In 2014, the album was preserved in the American National Recording Registry by the Library of Congress.

A 1997 remaster by Mobile Fidelity contained a slightly different version of the album. U2 celebrated the twentieth anniversary in 2007, releasing a remaster of the album completed by The Edge, including a bonus audio disc. In 2017, that remaster was released again but added additional remixes and new live material.

The thirtieth anniversary saw U2 touring *The Joshua Tree*, playing the album in full nightly. The tour visited North America, South America, and Europe in 2017. In 2019, the tour continued in Japan, Australia, and New Zealand. U2 also performed in Singapore, South Korea, the Philippines, and India for the first time. Concerts in Mexico were filmed by Anton Corbijn but remain unreleased at this time.

"WHERE THE STREETS HAVE NO NAME"

Lyrics: Bono
Music: U2
Producer: Lanois/Eno

"Where the Streets Have No Name" was developed at the end of the recording sessions. U2 struggled with the song, and after weeks of frustration Eno attempted to erase the master tapes, hoping to force U2 to start over. Pat McCarthy, the engineer, jumped in to prevent Eno from destroying the work.

The lyrics are inspired by Belfast where one's religion and income are said to be known based on what street they lived, and the anonymity that Bono felt during his visits to Ethiopia where there are no such barriers. Bono said, "I often feel very claustrophobic in a city, a feeling of wanting to break out of that city, and a feeling of wanting to go somewhere where the values of the city and the values of our society don't hold you down."[2]

The song was the third single, charting at #4 in the UK and #13 on the *Billboard* Hot 100 in the USA. The single featured a new mix, adding backing vocals by The Edge. A video directed by Meiert Avis was filmed at an impromptu concert on the roof of a liquor store in Los Angeles. It opens with a radio announcer talking about the surprise concert. U2's performance comprises most of the footage, with shots of the crowded streets and footage of Los Angeles police officers interacting with U2's crew and insisting that the production be shut down due to security concerns. The video won a Grammy Award for Best Performance Music Video at the 1989 Awards.

An edited version of the album recording is used on the compilation *U218 Singles*. The "High Contrast Remix" featured at the Athlete's Parade at the 2012 Olympic Games and released on the *Isles of Wonder* album. The "Flood Remix" released on the thirtieth anniversary collection includes alternate lyrics.

In concert, "Where the Streets Have No Name" is a U2 warhorse, being played at most shows since it debuted (it did take a break for the 2018 tour). Visually U2 has used red screens for the song since the original Joshua Tree Tour, highlighted in *Rattle and Hum*. The red screens even appeared when The Edge played the song with Muse at Glastonbury the year U2 cancelled due to Bono's back injury.

The Pet Shop Boys released their own cover of "Where the Streets Have No Name" which was mixed with a cover of "I Can't Take My Eyes Off of You." The cover reached #4 in the UK Charts, the same position that U2's own version had reached.

"Where the Streets Have No Name" was U2's seventh most streamed song at the end of 2021 on Spotify.

The song is celebrated in the fan community. One group of fans bring their own glitter to throw into the sky during performances. U2 have noticed the love for the song, and Bono shared, "We can be in the middle of the worst gig in our lives, but when we go into that song, everything changes. The audience is on its feet, singing along with every word. It's like God suddenly walks through the room. It's the point where craft ends, and spirit begins. How else do you explain it?"[3]

"I STILL HAVEN'T FOUND WHAT I'M LOOKING FOR"
Lyrics: Bono
Music: U2
Producer: Lanois/Eno

The Edge shares "'I Still Haven't Found What I'm Looking For' sounds like a song of defeat, but it's about hope and belief. God forbid if we ever found what we were looking for. What a horrible experience that would be."[4] The song started life under the name "Weather Girls."

Released as the second single, the song reached #6 in the UK and #1 in the USA. A video directed by Barry Devlin was filmed in Las Vegas following U2's concert in that city, depicting U2 wandering around Fremont Street, interacting with bystanders while The Edge plays an acoustic guitar. The video was credited with improving the image of Las Vegas for musicians and opening the city to wider interest among touring musical acts.

An alternate mix done by Lillywhite in 1987 was included in the thirtieth anniversary collection. Other mixes were released on *Earthrise: The Rainforest Album* (featuring added nature sounds) and *Rhythms Del Mundo Cuba* (featuring vocals by Coco Freeman).

Negativeland released a cover of the song in 1991 featuring lyrics of the song, mixed with outtakes from Casey Kasem's *American Top 40* program. The single was released under the title "U2." Island Records launched a lawsuit claiming Negativeland violated trademark with the use of the U2 name, and suggested they were acting to deliberately confuse U2 fans. Other covers have included versions by Celtic Thunder, Bonnie Tyler, and Cher. Cher frequently opened concerts with the song and has released the song as part of live performances.

In 2021, Bono and actress Scarlett Johansson recorded a new version for the animated film *Sing 2*. In the film, Bono voices an aged rock star who retired from music after the loss of his wife. Hearing the crowd sing this song draws him back for his first performance in years. The original U2 version of the song has also featured in several films including *Killing Bono, Runaway Bride,* and *Blown Away.* As one of U2's best-known songs, it appears frequently in concert. In 2015, during one performance, The Edge missed what he was looking for and fell off the stage during the song. Thankfully he was OK.

The song was nominated, but did not win, Record of the Year and Song of the Year at the 1988 Grammy Awards. The song was listed a #120 on Songs of the Century by the Recording Industry Association of America. *Q Magazine* listed it as #148 on a list of 1001 Best Songs Ever (2003). And *Rolling Stone* placed it on the 500 Greatest Songs of All Time (#93 in both 2004 and 2010). The song was U2's second most streamed song at the end of 2021 on Spotify.

"WITH OR WITHOUT YOU"
Lyrics: Bono
Music: U2
Producer: Lanois/Eno

Bono shares, "To me there's nothing more radical, there's nothing more revolutionary than two people loving each other. One, 'cause it's so uncommon these days, and two, 'cause it's so difficult to do."[5] "With or Without You" developed during The Unforgettable Fire Tour. U2 struggled with the song, and Gavin Friday and Bono took it away to work on it when the band was ready to abandon the song. A breakthrough came when The Edge was given a prototype Infinite Guitar by its inventor, used on the track.

It was the first single released, and U2's first #1 in the US. It reached #4 in the UK charts.

A video directed by Matt Mahurin is in black-and-white and uses very dark band performance footage mixed with footage of a nude dancer throughout. The woman is Morleigh Steinberg, a professional dancer and choreographer, filmed separately from U2. U2 would not meet her until 1993, when she took over the role of belly dancer on The Zoo TV Tour. She would marry The Edge in June 2002. A more common second video used some of the footage shot by Mahurin, but featured new performance elements shot by Meiert Avis, featuring U2 in both black-and-white and colour.

A remix by Daniel Lanois featured on the thirtieth anniversary collection is the only alternate studio version of the song. *Rolling Stone* placed the song on their Greatest Songs of All Time list (#131 in 2004, #132 in 2010) and on their 100 Greatest Pop Songs at #8 in 2010. *Q Magazine* listed the song at #17 on their 100 Greatest Songs of All Time (2006). The song was U2's most streamed song at the end of 2021 on Spotify.

In 2004, U2 reached #1 in the UK charts when British group LMC sampled "With or Without You" for their song "Take Me to the Clouds Above" using the lyrics from Whitney Houston's "How Will I Know." The song was released under the name LMC vs U2.

In 2001, looking back on the song after 9/11, Bono stated, "There's a lot of stuff that goes through your head, and the songs can completely change their meanings. Something like 'With or Without You' becomes about your audience. It's wild how a song can change."[6]

"With or Without You" has been covered by several artists over the years including Heaven 17 and Keane.

"Bullet the Blue Sky"
Lyrics: Bono
Music: U2
Producer: Lanois/Eno

Bono visited El Salvador during a civil war in 1986 meeting with a group helping refugees from the war. "Bullet the Blue Sky" was written about his experiences there:

> We went out into the hills. Maybe that was irresponsible. I don't know. Because we are in the middle of a warzone. I don't think it was that dangerous where we were. Some shots fired over our heads. The sound of gunfire in the open is very unromantic.[7]

Bono was not in immediate danger but close enough to worry. "When I explained to Edge what I had been through in El Salvador, he was able to, with a nod to Jimi Hendrix actually, put some of that fear and loathing into his guitar solo. We strapped my feelings to the song."[8]

The anger in the song carries into live performances. It has been performed at most concerts since 1987 and the performances through the years were featured in the 2017 tour program. A lyric from the song would provide the name for their next album, *Rattle and Hum*. For the thirtieth anniversary, a new remix by Jacknife Lee was released. Several live performances of the song have been released over the years, but this was the only other studio mix of the song to date.

"Running to Stand Still"
Lyrics: Bono
Music: U2
Producer: Lanois/Eno

On "Running to Stand Still" Bono returns to a topic from the previous album, "It was about a heroin problem in Dublin. The seven towers in the song is the place just behind where I grew up, what you call a housing project, with seven high towers."[9] The towers, Ballymun Towers, were built in the 1960s and used to house people moved out of the inner city. There were reports of many social problems among those living at the towers. The towers have all been demolished, with the last being removed in 2015. Daniel Lanois credited the song title to Bono's brother Norman, referring to running his business just to pay the bills.[10]

Bono has called the song one of his favourites, in his personal Top 5, when interviewed in late 1993.[11] A single remix of the song exists, done by Daniel Lanois for the thirtieth anniversary edition. "Running to Stand Still" provides some quiet after the audio barrage of "Bullet the Blue Sky" both on the album and often in concert.

British rock group Elbow covered the song for the War Child charity in 2008. The 7-inch had U2's version on one side, and Elbow's on the other. Guy Garvey, lead singer of Elbow, remembers "the excitement every time a U2 album was released, we just loved them. The first song we ever covered together before we had enough of our own songs to do a performance was 'Running to Stand Still'."[12]

As 2021 ended, Bono joined Glen Hansard and several other Irish artists for a busk to raise money for Simon Community, an organization helping the homeless in Ireland. Bono gave a beautiful performance of "Running to Stand Still" at St Patrick's Cathedral in Dublin. An album from the performances was released in 2022.

Actor Jeremy Piven names "Running to Stand Still" as one of his favourite U2 songs. Actor Ewan McGregor also calls it a favourite and performed an acoustic version on the television show *Long Way Round*.

"RED HILL MINING TOWN"
Lyrics: Bono
Music: U2
Producer: Lanois/Eno

In 1984, the National Union of Mineworkers opposed closures of mines in England, declaring a strike, leading to stresses in the communities affected. Bono shared:

> I was interested in the miners' strike politically, but I wanted to write about it on a more personal level. A cold statistic about a pit closure and redundancies that follow is drastic enough on one level, but it never tells the full human story. I wanted to follow the miner home and write about that situation in the song.[13]

The song was planned for the second single, but Bono discovered he had difficulty singing "Red Hill Mining Town," and the band chose "I Still Haven't Found" as the single instead. A video had been filmed with director Neil Jordan, featuring U2 performing in a coal mine but U2 were unhappy with the video, leaving it unreleased for twenty years.

The song features the Arklow Silver Band; however, the recording was not quite what U2 wanted, and they were mixed low in the original mix. For the thirtieth anniversary, Steve Lillywhite provided a new mix of the song, restoring the band to a more prominent place in the track. U2 released the new mix of "Red Hill Mining Town" as a single. Arklow Silver Band members share that the song was still called "The Eejit" when they recorded.

Due to the difficulties performing the song it never appeared in 1987, and for thirty years had not been performed live. The first performance was on the opening night of The Joshua Tree Tour 2017 tour. A live version from that tour was released on *The Joshua Tree New Roots* album, an album of other artists covering the songs from *The Joshua Tree*.

"In God's Country"
Lyrics: Bono
Music: U2
Producer: Lanois/Eno

"In God's Country" was about the American Dream, Bono says "I didn't know whether I was writing about Ireland or America for a while. Eventually I dedicated the song to the Statue of Liberty.... I wanted to write about America, and you know … the dream. The American dream."[14]

The song was released as the fourth single, but only in North America. It reached #44 in the US, and even managed to chart in the UK as an import single at #48. A video, directed by Barry Devlin, was used in the MTV documentary *Outside It's America*. Footage of Bono, decked out in denim and performing the song in a deserted manufacturing facility on acoustic guitar, is mixed with images from the 1930s and '40s of children, miners, steel factories, and soldiers. Additional footage includes city lights in colour and famous United States locations such as the Statue of Liberty, Mount Rushmore, and Times Square. The other members of U2 do not appear in the video.

After the Joshua Tree Tour in 1987, the song was played just eight times until the thirtieth anniversary tour.

"Trip Through Your Wires"
Lyrics: Bono
Music: U2
Producer: Lanois/Eno

U2 performed "Trip Through Your Wires" on *TV Gaga* in 1986 with very different lyrics. It was the first preview of the album, featuring Bono on harmonica. The song has only appeared live during The Joshua Tree Tours (1987, 2017 and 2019). The song is about a woman who captures a man in her "wires." Bono claims the song fits with "The Sweetest Thing"; a song written for his wife Ali. In concert in 2017, the song was accompanied by footage of The Edge's wife Morleigh on the screens.

In Australia, a 12-inch release of the song were hand-numbered and distributed to members of the music industry and stores that had supported the album. The version numbered from 1–100 is identified as one of the Top 60 U2 Collectibles by *Record Collector* magazine.

"One Tree Hill"
Lyrics: Bono
Music: U2
Producer: Lanois/Eno

Greg Carroll was a musician and producer and worked the local crew when U2 visited New Zealand in 1984. U2 saw a spark in him, Bono said, "My first night in New Zealand, Greg took me to One Tree Hill. He'd worked around the music and media scene and Paul McGuinness thought this guy's so smart, we can't leave him here, let's take him with us to Australia."[15] One Tree Hill is a volcanic peak in Auckland, an important memorial site for the Maori people.

In 1986, while running errands for Bono, Carroll was killed in a motorcycle accident. U2 were devastated. Larry, Bono, and Ali attended his funeral. The album is dedicated to Greg, and "One Tree Hill" was written for Carroll.

The song was released as the fourth single in Australia and New Zealand. It spent six weeks at #1 in New Zealand. A local television station, TVNZ, compiled footage of U2 with Greg Carroll combining it with scenic footage from New Zealand, including shots of One Tree Hill. As this was not an official video commissioned by U2, it has never been commercially released.

For the thirtieth anniversary collection, two new mixes of "One Tree Hill" were done, one by Brian Eno and the other by St Francis Hotel.

"Exit"
Lyrics: Bono
Music: U2
Producer: Lanois/Eno

Bono had been reading Norman Mailer's *Executioner's Song*, about the execution of a murderer in Utah, and other books that covered similar ground. "Exit" was recorded on the final day of recording. Bono wanted to explore the darker side of the American dream. Bono says:

> I don't even know what the act is in "Exit." Some see it as murder, others a suicide, and I don't mind. The rhythm of the words is nearly as important in conveying the state of mind. The album's real strength is that though you travel through

these deep tunnels and bleak landscapes, there's a joy at the heart of it, and I can't explain it.[16]

Introducing the song in concert, Bono calls it as "a song about a religious man, a fanatic, who gets into his head an idea he calls 'the hands of love'."[17]

The song was retired from live performances after the original album tour, except for one performance on the LoveTown Tour. The song was not performed live again until the 2017 tour. The song is full of darkness, and Bono frequently sings the song in character. During the 2017 and 2019 tour, the song was performed by Bono in character as "The Shadow Man."

Heavy metal group Anthrax did a faithful cover of "Exit" on their 2003 single "Taking the Music Back."

"MOTHERS OF THE DISAPPEARED"
Lyrics: Bono
Music: U2
Producer: Lanois/Eno

"Mothers of the Disappeared" refers to the human rights group Mothers of the Plaza de Mayo. This group of mothers of missing children had joined together to protest in Plaza de Mayo, in front of the presidential palace in Buenos Aires. Their children had been hunted down for their political views which dissented with the Argentine government. Bono met with some members of a similar group during his visit to Central America in 1986, "In my trip to Salvador I met with mothers of children who had disappeared. They have never found their children went or where their bodies were buried. They are presumed dead."[18]

Bono said, "It's not my position to lecture them or tell them their place or to even open their eyes up to it in a very visual way, but it is affecting me, and it affects the words I write and the music we make."[19]

The song was only performed at seven shows in 1987. It reappeared in Argentina and Chile in 1998 and 2005, with U2 bringing the Mothers on stage during a show in Buenos Aires in 1998. While touring Argentina Bono recorded an acapella version of the song in English, as well as reading the lyrics in Spanish. Both were used on an album compiled to commemorate twenty years of the Mothers of the Plaza de Mayo.

Extras from the Era

Bono states "With or Without You" is incomplete without the B-sides, all three songs seem to discuss different aspects of a relationship. "Walk to the Water" includes a line speaking about a suitcase full of unnecessary things, an early precursor to ideas explored in "Walk On." The other song is "Luminous Times (Hold on to Love)." "Walk to the Water" was rehearsed live in advance of the concert captured in colour for the *Rattle and Hum* film but was not played that night. A few lines were included in a performance in 2017 at Abbey Road Studios.

"Deep in the Heart" shares memories Bono had of the home he lived in at Cedarwood Road, which had recently been sold. There are references to the house and the street name in the lyric. One lyric reappeared years later in "Cedarwood Road." "Spanish Eyes" was not finished in time to include on the album. It received a video courtesy of the *Outside It's America* documentary, featuring footage of U2 travelling through Nevada, California, New Mexico, and Texas. For a B-side, it has gotten significant play live, mostly in concerts in Spain or Mexico. It was written for Bono's wife Ali and has been dedicated to her in concert. Legends say that the dark-haired, dark-eyed Irish are descendants of Spanish traders who settled in Ireland. Both songs appear on the "I Still Haven't Found What I'm Looking For" single.

"Where the Streets Have No Name" is backed with "Silver and Gold," "Sweetest Thing," and "Race Against Time." "Silver and Gold" was written for the *Sun City* album that Little Steven was putting together protesting Apartheid in Africa. Bono, inspired by the other artists he had met recording "Sun City," wrote his own for the album recording it with Keith Richards and Ron Wood of the Rolling Stones. Here, the song is recorded by U2. Like "Spanish Eyes" the song was played on The Joshua Tree Tour. "Race Against Time" has few words beyond the title of the song itself, essentially an instrumental.

"Sweetest Thing" was written for Ali when Bono missed her birthday in 1986. The song, rerecorded in 1998, was released as a single to promote *The Best of 1980–1990*, U2's first collection of hits. The single hit #3 in the UK and #63 in the US. A video to accompany the song, filmed by Kevin Godley, featured Bono and Ali riding in a carriage, while a street carnival breaks out around them, including banners saying "I'm Sorry," Boyzone, boxer Steve Collins, and more. Proceeds from the single were given to The Children of Chernobyl.

Five additional songs from the era were released on the twentieth anniversary deluxe release. "Wave of Sorrow" was little more than an instrumental piece called "Birdland" when abandoned in 1987. U2 recorded new music in 2007 including new vocals by Bono. "Drunk Chicken/America" was another song that featured new material recorded in 2007. The track features a reading by controversial American poet Allen Ginsberg. "Beautiful Ghost" features Bono reading William Blake's "Introduction to the Songs of Experience" over a U2 composition. "Desert of Our Love" and "Rise Up" are both early demos which appear here in the form they were left in 1986, with barely formed lyrics.

Two songs were also recorded with Canadian rock musician Robbie Robertson. They featured on his self-titled album. "Sweet Fire of Love" and "Testimony" feature the full band, recorded with Lanois in Dublin. Several remixes of "Testimony" also exist.

Rattle and Hum (1988)

Rattle and Hum was a combination of new material and live performances, released as the soundtrack to the film of the same name. The album was released October 10, 1988 and included nine new songs, six live performances, and two songs not even by U2. *Rattle and Hum* was U2's explorations of America throughout The Joshua Tree Tour. At one point the working name for the movie was *U2 in the Americas*. The live material captured here was filmed and recorded during The Joshua Tree Tour. Black and white footage was from Denver's McNichols Sports Arena over two nights. Colour footage from the tour was filmed during the band's concerts in Tempe Arizona a month later. The new songs were recorded in Dublin, Los Angeles, and Memphis. Overall, it is Jimmy Iovine who is credited as producer for the album.

The cover of the album is inspired by a scene in the film. It is not taken from the film but was recreated in studio by Anton Corbijn. The design of the album was handled by DZN, the Design group, chosen by Paramount Pictures to handle design for the film and album. It was the first album where Steve Averill did not contribute to the design; however, he would work on the singles released from the album.

The album reached #1 in both the UK and the US Charts and received good reviews. The film, however, did not garner the same positive reviews.

A remaster of the album has been released on iTunes, with mastering overseen by The Edge in 2017. It has not been released in additional formats at this time. A 2018 concert at the Apollo Theatre took a moment to celebrate the thirtieth anniversary of the album, with U2 being joined on stage by the Sun Ra Arkestra, to perform "Angel of Harlem," "Desire," and "When Love Comes to Town." The segment was directed by Hal Willner, a long-time collaborator of U2.

"HELTER SKELTER"
Lyrics: John Lennon/Paul McCartney
Producer: Jimmy Iovine

The album opens with a live performance of The Beatles' "Helter Skelter" recorded in Denver. The Beatles released the song in 1968 on *The Beatles*. The song had been interpreted by cult leader Charles Manson and used in his teachings, leading to Bono's impassioned introduction on the album. Adam Clayton spoke about including covers, "We get up on stage and we play some of those songs. And it's about playing those songs on that night whether or not you've rehearsed the thing. Rock'n'roll is something that's kind of passed on from one person to another. Through a few chords hummed. And that's what we were trying to do with this record."[1]

"VAN DIEMEN'S LAND"
Lyrics: The Edge
Music: U2
Producer: Jimmy Iovine

"Van Diemen's Land" borrows traditional elements from an old folk song called "The Water is Wide" but the lyric is new, written by The Edge. The Edge also appears on vocals. The song is "dedicated to John Boyle O'Reilly, a Fenian poet deported from Ireland to Australia because of his poetry. (It wasn't very good...!)" O'Reilly was a poet and journalist. He was initially deported to Australia for being a Fenian (seeking to establish an Irish Republic). He later escaped and settled in Boston. O'Reilly's life inspired the lyrics of the song.

The Edge explains:

It's based around coming upon the monument to the birthplace of John Boyle O'Reilly, the Irish poet, just about 25 miles north of Dublin. I never heard of the guy, I was just walking away, when I noticed in the window of what obviously some sort of ticket office when this place was open to the public some years ago. This faded brown newspaper clipping of his life. He was a Fenian, a man who believed in freedom for his country, and was sent away for expressing it in poetry. That theme of immigration, of the Irish artists leaving the country is something we as a band have felt at times. And we've seen so many other artists leaving Ireland.[2]

The song debuted in Australia and was played throughout the LoveTown Tour and at a handful of shows on the Zoo TV Tour. The most recent performance was when Bono and The Edge gave the first performance in the O2 arena in Dublin. The venue had once been the Point Depot where U2 recorded "Desire" and "Van Diemen's Land," and these are the two songs that Bono and The Edge played that night.

"Desire"
Lyrics: Bono
Music: U2
Producer: Jimmy Iovine

"Desire" features a beat influenced by Bo Diddley, by way of the Stooges song "1969." In the film we see U2 working on "Desire" at Point Depot. It is a demo recorded at STS Studios in Dublin on the album. U2 attempted to record it again in A&M Studios, but Adam Clayton claims, "We never did it better."[3]
Bono shares:

> The rhythm is the sex of the music. I wanted to own up to the religiosity of rock'n'roll concerts and the fact that you get paid for them. On one level, I'm criticizing the lunatic fringe preachers "stealing hearts at a travelling show" but I'm also starting to realize there's a real parallel between what I am doing and what they do. The song marries images of the big city, bright lights, heroin. It's about ambition. It's about wanting to be in a band. It's about wanting to be in a band for all the wrong reasons, not all the right reasons. It's about lust. It's about the lust for success.[4]

"Desire" was the first single and gave U2 their first #1 in the UK charts. In the US, they reached #3 on the Hot 100, #1 on the Alternative Songs chart, and even reached #37 on the Dance/Chart Play on the strength of the remix.

A video for "Desire," filmed by Richard Lowenstein in Los Angeles features U2 in LA, black-and-white footage of them playing in-studio, and excerpts from local news casts. Bono can be seen on the roof of the Rosslyn Hotel in the footage. A longer edit of the video is set to the Hollywood Remix.

The "Hollywood Remix" was five minutes long, but a nine-minute version was released for promotion. Backing vocals on the remix were provided by Edna Wright (former lead singer of Honey Cone and younger sister of Darlene Love) and Alexandra Brown (a member of the Raeletts, the backing band for Ray Charles).

The song was named #675 on the 1000 Best Songs Ever by *Q Magazine* in 2003. And "Desire" won U2 a Grammy Award for Best Rock Performance by a Duo or Group at the 1989 awards.

"Hawkmoon 269"
Lyrics: Bono
Music: U2
Producer: Jimmy Iovine

"Hawkmoon 269" features Bob Dylan on Hammond Organ, his first appearance on the album. Backing vocals are by Edna Wright and Carolyn Willis (from the girl group Honey Comb) and Billie Barnum (from the girl group The Apollas). The song was recorded in Hollywood, CA, at Sunset Sound studios.

Hawkmoon is mentioned in the lyric of the song. In *U2 by U2*, The Edge identifies this as a place in Rapid City, South Dakota, however there is no such place in South Dakota.[5] Blackhawk does exist on the outskirts of Rapid City. The Edge suggests the 269 came from the number of the mixes of the song that were completed.

Bono suggests it is not a real place, "I called it Hawkmoon 269 because, well it's a reference to a few people, one of my favorite writers, Sam Shepard, but also it's a motel room in my imagination somewhere. The 269 isn't a motel room number but it's the fact we mixed it 269 times before we got it right. We're that professional man! I think it's probably the greatest rock'n'roll we recorded, the most abandoned anyway."[6]

Actor and musician Steven Van Zandt has named "Hawkmoon 269" as one of his favourite U2 songs.

"ALL ALONG THE WATCHTOWER"
Lyrics: Bob Dylan
Producer: Jimmy Iovine

U2's performance of Dylan's "All Along the Watchtower" was taken from a free lunch time concert held in San Francisco, the "Save the Yuppie Free Concert." During the show, Bono spray-painted "Rock n' Roll Stops the Traffic" on the Vaillancourt Fountain, earning him a fine. Larry revealed, "It was the first time we played it live and we put it in the movie."[7] Dylan's version was released in 1967 on *John Wesley Harding*.

"I STILL HAVEN'T FOUND WHAT I'M LOOKING FOR"
Lyrics: Bono
Music: U2
Producer: Jimmy Iovine

U2 performs with gospel choir The New Voices of Freedom in New York City. An alternate version of the song can be seen in the film, shot during rehearsal at a church in Harlem ahead of the concert. The gospel choir had been approached by Island Records to record their own version of the song with plans to release it after U2's version peaked in the charts. Island Records founder Chris Blackwell put a stop to the plan worried it would look like a money-grab. Although not released by Island, the song did reach U2, and they invited the choir to join them on stage in New York.

"Freedom for My People"
Lyrics: Sterling Magee/Bobby Robinson/Macie Mabins

"Freedom for My People" is a short performance by two busking musicians—Adam Gussow and Sterling Magee. The performers, known as Satan and Adam, busked in Harlem through the 1980s and 1990s. They recorded several albums and in 2019 a documentary called *Satan & Adam* includes a cameo by The Edge. Magee passed away due to complications from COVID-19 in September 2020.

"Silver and Gold"
Lyrics: Bono
Music: U2
Producer: Jimmy Iovine

U2 perform "Silver and Gold" in Denver. The song was originally recorded solo by Bono for the *Sun City* album and later recorded by U2 as a B-side for "Where the Streets Have No Name."

"Pride (In the Name of Love)"
Lyrics: Bono
Music: U2
Producer: Jimmy Iovine

U2 perform "Pride (In the Name of Love)" in Denver. The song is the final performance from the Denver concert used on the album. In the film "Exit," "In God's Country," "Bad," and "Sunday Bloody Sunday" from that concert are also included, but they do not appear on the soundtrack.

"Angel of Harlem"
Lyrics: Bono
Music: U2
Producer: Jimmy Iovine

"Angel of Harlem" was written for jazz singer Billie Holiday ("Lady Day"). Bono recalled, "We're still fans of the greats, from Elvis Presley and Billie Holiday to Bob Dylan to the Band to the Waterboys to whoever."[8] The song recalls when U2 first visited New York, travelling into the city and hearing Billie Holiday on the radio. Bono remembers:

My first impression, I suppose it's an impression shared by all of us in the band was a naive one, a very romantic idea of what America was, and what New York was. The mood of the song seems to suit that. Coming over and into Manhattan, I'd never seen anything quite like that. I suppose I should sound a bit jaded and play it very cool on that front. But it wasn't. It was a real thrill, a thrill I'll never forget. There was music on the radio, we were just turning the dial, I heard a voice I don't know what song it was. I just said who's that and the driver said "that's Billie Holiday." I'd never even heard of Billie Holiday.[9]

The song was written while touring and recorded in Memphis. "When Love Comes to Town," "Love Rescue Me," "She's a Mystery to Me" (unreleased), "Can't Help Falling in Love" (unreleased), and "Jesus Christ" were all recorded during those sessions at Sun Studios, a famous studio where Elvis Presley, Roy Orbison, Johnny Cash, and others had recorded throughout their careers.

"Angel of Harlem" was released as the second single and the release featured an image of Billie Holiday on the back. The single version is a remix, with several subtle differences, the horns are sharper, and Bono's vocals are doubled in places. The single reached #9 in the UK charts, and reached #14 in the USA on the Hot 100, and #3 on the Alternative Songs chart.

"Angel of Harlem" was nominated for Best Song Written Specifically for a Motion Picture at the 1990 Grammy Awards but did not win the award.

A video filmed by director Richard Lowenstein includes footage of U2 performing at the Apollo Theatre in New York City and scenes of New York City, footage of U2 attending the premiere of *Rattle and Hum* in New York and Los Angeles and old footage of Billie Holiday. The film features video of the recording sessions at Sun Studios including alternate lyrics that did not make the final song.

"LOVE RESCUE ME"
Lyrics: Bono and Bob Dylan
Music: U2
Producer: Jimmy Iovine

Bono woke up with "Love Rescue Me" in his head. He reached out to Bob Dylan, thinking the ideas were from a Dylan song. Dylan confirmed it was not and the two worked on lyrics for the song together. Dylan also provides backing vocals on the song. Originally a lead vocal by Dylan was recorded but, in the end, it was not used.

"Love Rescue Me" was completed at Sun Studios. U2 had been looking to do some recording and had reached out to Jimmy Iovine to arrange a studio. Adam Clayton shared:

Sun had been closed for the last ten years or something, I don't know how Jimmy did it, but he just got us in there. Sun just had that vibe. It was a small place. It wasn't that high tech thing that recording has become, where people make records rather than make music. Sun had its history. It was a room where you felt comfortable. You had to listen to what you were doing.[10]

"When Love Comes to Town"
Lyrics: Bono
Music: U2
Producer: Jimmy Iovine

B.B. King performed at the National Stadium in Dublin and Bono was in attendance, sharing:

I was blown away by the way he sang, when he moved back from the microphone his voice got louder. I had to go backstage to ask him how you do that trick. He knows he's a great guitar player, but he really seems to underestimate how great a singer he is. I told him. He asked me to produce his next record, I said I wouldn't be interested in that, but I'd write a song for him.[11]

Bono wrote the first two verses right away but wrote the other verses just before meeting King again. In the film we see B.B. King working with U2 live during a soundcheck. The version on the album was recorded at Sun Studios.

The song was the third single. Singles contained the album version or an edit. The "Live from the Kingdom Mix" on the single is treated so it sounds as if it was recorded in concert. The remix adds a saxophone solo by Dave Koz, and a sermon by Little Richard. Multiple edits of the remix exist.

The first video was taken directly from the film, and featured U2 and B.B. King rehearsing the song and performing it live—both a long and a short edit exist. A second video used footage filmed for the movie, but not just the scenes with King. We see scenes shot throughout the US with footage from Memphis, Austin, New York and St Louis as well as several unidentified rural locations.

B.B. King toured with U2 on the LoveTown Tour, joining U2 on stage for performances of this song with his band. King has released live versions of the song recorded without U2 on *Live at the Apollo* and *B.B. King Live*. U2 have often played the song without King as well. When King died as U2 were starting their tour in 2015 U2 incorporated the song in several shows at the start of the tour.

"When Love Comes to Town" was nominated for Best Rock Performance by a Duo or Group with Vocal at the 1990 Grammy Awards, but did not win.

"Heartland"

Words: Bono
Music: U2
Producer: Jimmy Iovine

"Heartland" was started during *The Unforgettable Fire* sessions and finished during sessions for *The Joshua Tree*. It was left off the album in favour of "Trip Through Your Wires." Bono and Adam had visited Daniel Lanois at his home studio in New Orleans, "New Orleans had the sweetness of a rotting vine when the grapes are just on the turn. I loved it, the noble rot as wine lovers call it. There's some dark colours, violet and purple," Bono shared.[12] He said the lyrics for "Heartland" came out of a travelogue that was kept during that trip. The song was recorded by Kevin Killen and Lanois at Danesmoate in Dublin. Brian Eno appears on keyboards.

The song is the only song on the album that has not been performed live in concert. In 2020, Bono revealed that their tour film documenting the Joshua Tree 2017 Tour would be called *Heartland* and would include a performance of "Heartland" in the desert, filmed by Anton Corbijn. At this time the film has not been released.

"God Part II"

Lyrics: Bono
Music: U2
Producer: Jimmy Iovine

If *Rattle and Hum* was about looking back, "God Part II" showed us the direction that U2 were heading. Bono takes on Albert Goldman, the author who wrote *The Lives of John Lennon*. The 1988 book was a harsh look at Lennon, which many claimed damaged Lennon's legacy.

Bono shared:

> I objected to Albert Golddigger picking a fight on a dead man. Luckily enough he still lives on in his music, and his music has inspired us. We just became a voice. It was also an interesting way to exercise some of our own contradictions. Albert Goldman thought he was pointing out a great contradiction, trying to tell the world that John Lennon was very confused, crippled inside, and therefore less of a man for it. When the great thing about John Lennon was, he knew that he was, wrote songs about it, we certainly didn't need a book to take us further down that road.[13]

Lennon's song "God" was released on his first post-Beatles album recorded with the Plastic Ono Band. U2's lyrics include a nod to Canada's Bruce Cockburn.

The line Bono heard on the radio is taken from Cockburn's song "Lovers in a Dangerous Time."

"God Part II" was delivered to radio stations unlikely to play "When Love Comes to Town." There was also a remix of the song done by Lou Silal Jr., titled the Hard Metal Dance Mix. Two edits of that remix have been released over the years.

"THE STAR-SPANGLED BANNER"
Performed by Jimi Hendrix

"The Star-Spangled Banner" is a shortened version of Jimi Hendrix's performance of the American national anthem at the Woodstock Festival in 1969. It is included here as the introduction to "Bullet the Blue Sky."

"BULLET THE BLUE SKY"
Words: Bono
Music: U2
Producer: Jimmy Iovine

"Bullet the Blue Sky" is from a performance in Tempe, Arizona, filmed on the final night of the tour. It is the only song on the album taken from Tempe on the soundtrack album, but other performances are featured in the film including "MLK," "Where the Streets Have No Name," "With or Without You," and "Running to Stand Still."

"ALL I WANT IS YOU"
Words: Bono
Lyrics: U2
Producer: Jimmy Iovine

"All I Want is You" plays over the final credits of the film and ends with strings provided by Van Dyke Parks. An alternate vocal is featured on the album. The Edge says it "is probably the best of what we were trying to do with the album, in that it has a traditional basis, but it was a truly U2 song."[14] Bono speaking about the song often brings up his wife Ali. It is not a surprise she inspired the lyrics.

The song was released as the final single. A shortened four-minute edit was featured on the single. A pressing in green vinyl in Australia was listed by *Record Collector* magazine as the rarest U2 collectible, and it is thought there are less than ten copies.

U2 worked with director Meiert Avis to film a video near Rome. The video tells a story featuring a circus wintering on a beach with a brief appearance by U2. The story focuses on actors Paola Rinaldi and Paolo Risi. Rinaldi plays an aerial performer, and Risi plays a fellow circus worker who is enamored with her, although she is involved with another man. During the story someone dies, and it has been a matter of debate over the years as to who is buried. The Edge has gone on record as saying that it was the trapeze artist played by Rinaldi who died.

The song appears on the soundtrack to *Reality Bites* and in the movie *Contagion*. Irish pop group Bellefire had some chart success with their cover of the song, reaching #18 in the UK and #5 at home in Ireland.

Extras from the Era

Most of the B-sides accompanying the *Rattle and Hum* album were covers, which are listed in the Appendix. There were two original songs. "Hallelujah, Here She Comes" featured on the B-side of "Desire." Billy Preston joined U2 on the song on vocals and Hammond organ. Preston was a top session musician who had backed artists like The Beatles, Little Richard, and the Rolling Stones. "A Room at the Heartbreak Hotel" featured on "Angel of Harlem," Bono explained "It's about somebody who really wants to be a star. Everybody wants to live in Graceland. But nobody wants to die there."[15] Backing vocals on the song are provided by Maxine and Julia Waters, members of the family group The Waters. A shorter edit of both tracks appears on the bonus disc on *The Best of 1980–1990*.

7

Achtung Baby (1991)

Achtung Baby was recorded with Daniel Lanois and Brian Eno. Lanois acted as the primary producer, working full time with U2, while Eno would join them for a week at a time each month. Mark Ellis, aka Flood worked as an engineer on the sessions. Recording took U2 to Hansa Ton Studios in Berlin initially, just as the Berlin wall was coming down. U2 would spend a month in Berlin before returning home to finish the album, working at Dog Town, STS Studios, and Windmill Lane Studios in Dublin.

U2 were hoping to catch some excitement in Germany. The studio had been where many of their idols had recorded including David Bowie and Iggy Pop. The city was going through reunification. Instead, they found the city cold and struggled to find their path in the studio. U2 even verged on breaking up, but a breakthrough in the form of "One" gave them hope. In early 1991, U2 reported that the tapes from the Berlin sessions had been stolen and bootlegs of that material started to circulate before the album came out.

The title of the album was taken from the movie *The Producers*. The phrase, heard in the film, was used by sound engineer Joe O'Herlihy throughout the recording sessions in Berlin. The cover was designed by Steve Averill, working with Shaughn McGrath for the first time. Trying to steer clear of their covers from the 1980s, U2 used colour photographs, and instead of one larger image, set up a grid pattern using multiple images shot by Anton Corbijn during Carnival in Tenerife, in Morocco, and in Berlin, as well as some shots in studio in Dublin. The label of the CD features the first appearance of the cartoon "Achtung Baby," nicknamed Cosmo, featured on artwork throughout the 1990s. Alternate titles considered for the album included *Adam*, *Zoo Station*, *69*, and *Man*.

The album debuted at #1 in the US and #2 in the UK charts. The album is widely regarded as one of U2's finest. *Rolling Stone* has listed the album in its Top 500 Albums Poll (#62 in 2003, #63 in 2012, and #125 in 2020). *Spin* placed it at #11 in a list of the 100 Greatest Albums 1985–2005. The album is listed in Robert Dimery's book *1001 Albums You Must Hear Before You Die*. The album was nominated for

Grammy Awards, winning Best Rock Performance by a Duo/Group, but missing out on Album of the Year, losing out to Eric Clapton's *Unplugged*.

The album was reissued in 2011 for the twentieth anniversary. It was not remastered at that time. It was released in deluxe formats with six audio discs and four video discs. One of the audio discs was a demo recording of every song on the album, called "baby versions." A documentary by Davis Guggenheim was released as part of the packaged titled *From the Sky Down*. U2 also worked with *Q Magazine* to produce *(Ähk-toõng Bäy-Bi) Covered*, a compilation of covers of each track on the album.

A remaster under the guidance of The Edge was released on vinyl in 2018. In 2021, for the thirtieth anniversary, that remaster was issued as a digital box set and in coloured vinyl.

"Zoo Station"
Written by U2
Producer: Lanois

"Zoo Station" kicked off a new direction for U2. The Edge shared, "It's basically a very simplistic statement pronouncing that U2 was ready to come back out and strut our stuff. We went through a reclusive period and went off and did the family thing, which was the right thing. But now we are fresh. I can honestly say that all four of us are totally committed to *Achtung Baby* and the ZooTV tour."[1]

In Berlin, adjacent to the Zoo, is the Zoologischer Garten railway station, a stop connecting the U-Bahn subway line (known as the U2 since 1993, it was known as the U1 when U2 were recording) and S-Bahn line. Anton Corbijn described the station as "the famous station in West Berlin that went to the East. It's a legendary type of station. It was a point of arrival or departure..."[2] Before the Berlin Wall came down in 1989, if one wanted to travel to East Berlin by train, you went via Zoo Station.

The song was born out of "Lady with the Spinning Head." An instrumental remix of the song was included on the "Miss Sarajevo" single under the name "Bottoms (Watashitachi No Ookina Yuma)." "Zoo Station" was issued as a promotional picture disc to promote the ZooTV Tour.

Nine Inch Nails contributed a cover of the song for a twentieth anniversary covers album.

"Even Better Than the Real Thing"
Written by U2
Producer: Lillywhite with Eno/Lanois

"Even Better Than the Real Thing" developed during the sessions for *Rattle and Hum*. A demo was recorded at STS Studios when U2 recorded "Desire." U2 took it to Germany to work on at Hansa, finishing it in Dublin. The song was a statement on commercialism, with Bono revealing the song "is much more reflective of the times we were living in, when people were no longer looking for the truth, we are all looking for instant gratification. It's not substantial as a lyric but it suggests a certain sexual tension and desire to have some fun playing in the shallows."[3]

The song was issued as the fourth single including remixes of the song by Paul Oakenfold with Steve Osbourne and Apollo 440. The album and single versions both use the same vocal track, but the instrumentation is different in the two mixes and the single places greater emphasis on the vocals near the end.

The cover of the single fits together with three other *Achtung Baby* singles to make a larger image of U2 sitting in a Trabant ("Even Better Than the Real Thing" is the top left corner, "Who's Going to Ride Your Wild Horses" the top right, "Mysterious Ways" the bottom left, and "The Fly" the bottom right).

The single reached #12 in the UK charts for the main single and #8 for the remix single, issued a week later. In the US, the song reached #32. The remixes hit #27 on the Dance/Club Play Songs chart.

A video directed by Kevin Godley won MTV Video Music Awards in 1992 for "Best Special Effects" and "Best Group Video." It featured a unique 360-degree camera rig allowing for continual rotation around U2. The video also featured footage of a group of U2 impersonators, as well as television and video footage from a variety of sources. A second video, filmed by Armando Gallo, featured a collage of live shots taken from The ZooTV Tour, augmented by a variety of symbols flying across the screen. The final version of the video is the "Dance Remix," directed by Richie Smyth. It features footage of U2 in Santa Cruz for Carnival, participating in photo shoots for the *Achtung Baby* cover. That version is set to "The Perfecto Mix."

U2 contributed the "Jacques Lu Cont" mix of their own song for an album of covers for the twentieth anniversary of the album. A remix by "Fish Out of Water" was also produced for the anniversary collection.

"ONE"
Written by U2
Producer: Lanois with Eno

It has been mentioned in many recollections that U2 were miserable in Berlin, they did not know what they wanted to do, and they came very close to walking away from not only a new album, but from U2 itself. While working on an early version of "Ultra Violet," Daniel Lanois suggested marrying two pieces of music together, and Bono was inspired. Bono said the lyrics "just fell out of the sky, a gift from above."[4] The Edge shared that it was a breakthrough moment for U2, "Everyone recognized it was a crucial moment in the development of what became *Achtung*

Baby—ironically it went in a totally different direction from everything we'd been working on. But everyone recognized it was a special piece."[5]

Bono calls the song a conversation between father and son. The Edge explained on U2 X-Radio:

A great song operates on levels that defy explanation. For instance, one of our songs "One"—if you just looked at the lyric on a page it's pretty evident it's a very nasty row between family members. As we were putting the lyric together, we created this scenario in our heads between a gay young man and his father, who is having a really hard time dealing with his sexuality. It's a song about AIDS.[6]

Two remixes were commissioned in 1992 from Apollo 440, but they remained unreleased until the album was reissued in 2011.

The song was released as the third single. U2 went to long-time collaborator Anton Corbijn for a video for the song. Corbijn admits he was "emotionally hurt" when U2 turned the video down and went with other ideas instead.[7] The first video released was developed for tour screens, directed by Mark Pellington featured buffalo running, blooming flowers, and the word "One" translated into various languages. U2 also filmed black-and-white footage with Pellington creating another edit of his buffalo video. A video directed by Phil Joanou featured Bono sitting in a restaurant in New York City.

While these videos were released, Corbijn reworked his version which featured U2 in Hansa performing the song, Trabants driving in Berlin, Bono's father, and U2 in drag. The royalties for the song were being donated to AIDS research, and while happy with the initial video, The Edge explained:

We didn't want to be involved in putting back the AIDS issue into the realm of sexuality and all that because thank God it seems to have gone beyond that. It wasn't worth the risk of people imagining we were saying something about the AIDS issue through the drag footage which was totally not what we were trying to say. So unfortunately, we had to stop it.[8]

In 2005, Anton's original vision for the video was finally released.

The artwork on the single depicts a Native American hunting technique, of buffalo being run off a cliff. The photo was by David Wojnarowicz, who died a few months after the release of "One" because of AIDS-related complications. The cover reads, "Wojnarowicz identifies himself and ourselves with the buffalo, pushed into the unknown by forces we cannot control or even understand."

The song reached #10 in the USA and #1 on the Alternative charts. In the UK, it reached #7. *Q Magazine* named "One" #1 on a list of the 1001 Best Songs Ever in 2003, and again named it #1 on the 100 Greatest Songs of All Time in 2006. *Rolling Stone* listed it at #36 on its list of 500 Greatest Songs of All Times in their lists compiled in 2004 and 2010.

U2 performed a version of "One" with Mary J. Blige as part of the *Shelter from the Storm* telethon, held in the wake of Hurricane Katrina. Later that year, Mary J. Blige released her album *The Breakthrough* including the performance of "One" enhanced with additional instrumentation and an orchestra. Released as a single, it reached #2 on the UK Chart. A video directed by Paul Hunter, opens with footage of U2 performing while Mary J. Blige is transported to the venue, showing her arriving on stage in time to sing. The version recorded with Mary J. Blige was nominated, but did not win, for Best Pop Collaboration with Vocals at the 2007 Grammy Awards.

Of the many interpretations of the song, The Edge has said, "This song with all this hurt and vitriol is often now the song people decide to have played at their wedding. Situations where it would just be completely inappropriate. Except for the fact that there's some sort of powerful emotion in that combination of words and melody that is a new thing."[9] "One" is one of U2's most covered songs, covered by the Cowboy Junkies, Mica Paris, Joe Cocker, Johnny Cash, and many more. A performance by a band called Automatic Baby performing the song at MTV's Inaugural Ball for President Bill Clinton has been released on several charity compilations. The band was made up of Mike Mills and Michael Stipe from R.E.M. joined by Larry Mullen and Adam Clayton. The song was U2's third most streamed song at the end of 2021 on Spotify.

"One" has been called "the greatest song ever written" by Noel Gallagher.[10]

"Until the End of the World"
Written by U2
Producer: Lanois with Eno

"Until the End of the World" conveys the struggles between Jesus and Judas. The Edge explains, "There's an Irish poet named Brendan Kennelly who's written a book of poems about Judas. One of the lines is, 'If you want to serve the age, betray it.' That really set my head reeling. He's also fascinated with the whole moral concept of 'Where would we be without Judas?'"[11] Bono shares, "I played Jesus for so long, I decided I needed a break! Judas, from whatever way you look at it, is a fascinating creature, because in one sense, by committing his crime, he introduced us to Grace."[12]

The song has often been a centerpiece of live shows since the ZooTV Tour. Two earlier demos of the song featured in Wim Wenders movie *The End of the World*, one in the film and one on the soundtrack. As the film was released in Germany ahead of "The Fly" as a single, it gave a first peek of the album to come. A video for the song directed by Richie Smyth features U2 in various stages of undress, road movie footage from Wenders' film, and The Edge in plastic wrap.

Patti Smith contributed a lovely cover of the song to the twentieth anniversary covers collection.

"WHO'S GONNA RIDE YOUR WILD HORSES"
Written by U2
Producer: Lillywhite/Lanois/Eno

"Who's Gonna Ride Your Wild Horses" is about the end of a relationship, possibly The Edge's marriage, but Bono's lyrics often have many interpretations. The song was initially recorded during sessions at STS Studios in 1990. U2 would bring in Steve Lillywhite to mix the song for the album, a process that took more than a month to complete. Steve Lillywhite remembers "They hated that song. I spent a month on it and I still don't think it was as realized as it could've been. The Americans had heard it and said, 'That's your radio song there,' because they were having trouble with some of the more industrial elements."[13]

The song was the fifth single, released a year after the album. The album version was reworked into a new mix known as "The Temple Bar Remix" (and the more radio friendly "The Temple Bar Edit"). The remixes were done by U2 with Paul Barrett after U2 had some time to live with the song, and it ended up being their preferred version. Temple Bar refers to the area of Dublin where STS Studios was located where the remix was done. A version of the remix with added nature sounds was released on the *Earthrise II* compilation.

A video, filmed by Phil Joanou, features a collage of live footage from the ZooTV tour plus U2 miming to a recorded version of the song on a white background, set to the "Temple Bar Remix" of the song.

Garbage contributed a cover for the twentieth anniversary covers album incorporating samples of U2's original.

The song reached #35 in the USA and #14 in the UK.

"SO CRUEL"
Written by U2
Producer: Lanois

"So Cruel" is a dark song about the end of a relationship. Adam Clayton names it as his favourite song on the album. The song was developed in Dublin long after the Berlin sessions. It came together quickly. Nell Catchpole, a frequent collaborator of Brian Eno, joins U2 playing violin and viola on the track. Bono says the song "is mostly my song. I picked up a guitar late one night in Dogtown and started singing. People thought it was too traditional, one more attempt at writing a song for Roy Orbison but Flood found a way of making it feel like it was on the same album."[14]

Depeche Mode covers "So Cruel" on the twentieth anniversary covers collection.

"The Fly"
Written by U2
Producer: Lanois

Bono announced that The Fly was "the sound of four men chopping down *The Joshua Tree*."[15] The song debuted on radio ahead of the album release, giving most fans a first taste of the new sound. The Edge said the song was inspired by:

> These characters, certainly in Dublin and I'm sure everywhere else, who sit on these stools by the bar all day. And they know everything. They seem to have moles in the White House and seem to know exactly what's going on in Moscow. They're bar-stool philosophers, with all these great theories and notions. And they're on the edge of madness and genius.[16]

Bono's description of the character is a little more over the top, "The way I saw 'The Fly' was like an obscene phone call from Hell, but the guy likes it there. He's like calling home, saying, I like it."[17]

"The Fly" developed out of "Lady with the Spinning Head." The song was refined in Dublin, as Bono began forming ideas about the persona he would adopt in concert. That persona, known as "The Fly," would debut in a video directed by Jon Klein and Richie Smyth. In the video, filmed in Dublin and London, we see The Fly walking around the streets and footage of U2 in-studio performing the song. The song introduces several ZooTV concepts, including a bank of televisions, a scrolling sign saying, "Watch More TV," flashing words, and the ZooTV logo.

"The Fly" was issued as the first single. A mix of the song by Flood, called "The Lounge Fly Mix" with alternate lyrics was included. The single reached #61 in the US and reached #1 on the Alternative charts. In the UK, the song reached #1.

Longtime U2 friend Gavin Friday covered the song for the twentieth anniversary covers album and it was also used during the intermission at later shows on U2's 2015 tour. "The Fly" was covered by a parody act called The Joshua Trio, doing a country version of the song. The group even signed onto U2's record label, Mother, releasing a three-song single including "The Fly," "Where the Streets Have No Name," and "Bad." Bono called them a favourite act in *Rolling Stone*. The group included Arthur Matthews who would later co-create *Father Ted*, a beloved Irish television comedy.

"The Fly" made it to *Q Magazine*'s 2003 list of the 1001 Best Songs Ever, coming in at #875 on the list.

"Mysterious Ways"
Written by U2
Producer: Lanois with Eno

"Mysterious Ways" was initially called "Sick Puppy," the song was started in Berlin, and the band worked on it until the last minute, with guitar overdubs added after the final mix. The song is U2 at their funkiest according to Bono, "it's a song about a man living with little or no romance. We were going to call the album *Fear of Women* at one point."[18]

The song was the second single and featured remixes of the title track by Howard Gray, Trevor Gray and Steve Lillywhite, Apollo 440, Paul Oakenfold and Steve Osborne, and by The Stereo MCs. Another remix by Massive Attack would be released on the *Melon* fan club album. "Mysterious Ways" appeared on *The Best of 1990–2000* but using a different vocal with one line being completely different.

A video for "Mysterious Ways," filmed in Fez, Morocco, by Stéphane Sednaoui, featured street scenes in Morocco, including shots of Bono dancing, cobras writhing, and a belly dancer gyrating against a blue moon. Special effects were employed to warp the video images using mirrors.

The single reached #13 in the UK. In the USA, the song reached #9 on the Hot 100 chart, #42 on the Dance/Club Charts, and #1 on the Alternative songs.

"Mysterious Ways" has been covered by Snow Patrol, Angélique Kidjo, KMFDM, and many others.

"TRYIN' TO THROW YOUR ARMS AROUND THE WORLD"
Written by U2
Producer: Lanois with Eno

Bono shares, "It's a song about drunk ambition but in the funniest sense, not so much megalomania but just the ambition to get home in one piece. It was written in Australia, staying up all night and missing my baby."[19]

One of the most quoted lyrics from "Tryin' to Throw Your Arms Around the World" is not a Bono original. "A woman needs a man like a fish needs a bicycle" was a popular line during the feminist movement of the 1970s, coined by Irina Dunn, an Australian social activist.

A "baby" version of the song was released for the twentieth anniversary of the album, but unlike those released for other songs, additional work has been done recording new music to add to the original pieces. No other studio versions of the song have been released.

"ULTRA VIOLET (LIGHT MY WAY)"
Written by U2
Producer: Lanois with Eno

"Jealousy. Infidelity. Love rears its ugly head again."[20] That is Bono's description of "Ultra Violet." The song is one of those which developed out of "Lady with the Spinning Head," noted in the title of that demo as "UV1" or "Ultra Violet #1." U2 struggled with the song, and it was The Edge that worked out where to go with it on piano.

Adam Clayton shares, "It is a dark song that a lot of people really love. It touches a nerve It suggests infidelity. without being specific…. The title might have something to do with those stamps that you get on your hands when you go to a nightclub, that only show up under ultra violet light. If you tell your partner you were out working late, those stamps can bust you."[21]

The song has made a surprising number of appearances in recent tours. On the U2360° Tour, it was a centerpiece as Bono's jacket lit up and he swung from his microphone. It returned in 2017 and 2019 for The Joshua Tree tours, each night the screen lit up with women who had helped change history including politicians, protesters, scientists, and more. A total of 331 women were featured on screen throughout the tours.

A shortened edit of the song was sent to radio in the Philippines. The Killers covered the song for the twentieth anniversary covers album.

"ACROBAT"
Written by U2
Producer: Lanois

In 2005, Bono called "Acrobat" one of his favourite U2 songs, "it's a song about your own spleen, your own hypocrisy, your own ability to change shape and take on the colours of whatever environment you're in, like a chameleon."[22]

The song is dedicated to Delmore Schwartz, a writer who had been a big influence on Lou Reed. Bono borrowed the line "In dreams begin responsibilities" from the title of a short story written by Schwartz in 1935. The line is older still, as Schwartz had taken the title from W. B. Yeats' book *Responsibilities*, and Yeats had borrowed from an old play.[23]

Other than the "baby" version on the twentieth anniversary album, there are no other studio versions of the song. Although rehearsed for ZooTV, the song was never performed in concert on that tour, and until 2018 had not been played at all. In 2015, a fan-organized effort called #U2Request asked fans to name the song they desired to hear most in concert. Over 50,000 tweets were submitted by fans with "Acrobat" named as the most requested song. In 2018, at the opening night of U2's new tour, the song debuted live and would be played at every show. Maybe U2 did see those U2 Requests!

"LOVE IS BLINDNESS"
Written by U2
Producer: Lanois
Bono shared that "Love in Blindness" was "written for Nina Simone and we just started playing it one night and U2 liked it, so we decided to put it on the album. But the best thing about the record is Edge's guitar playing. To me, it's like a prayer."[24]
Although written with Simone in mind, the song may reflect on the breakdown of

The Edge's marriage. The Edge said, "A lot of people have read into the lyrics that it's the story of Edge's marriage breaking down. I'm not denying that that has had an influence, but I think there's a lot of stories in there and it's not just my story."[25]

A video directed by Matt Mahurin was released as part of the video single of "Numb." The video includes U2 performing during the ZooTV Tour, mixed with random images, including an empty park bench, waves crashing, a street busker playing accordion, and clouds in the sky.

"Love is Blindness" is performed acoustically by The Edge in the documentary, *From the Sky Down*.

Although Simone never released a version of the song, jazz singer Cassandra Wilson recorded her own version of the song. In 2016, a cover of the song by Lee-La Baum appeared in a commercial for an Yves Saint Laurent fragrance, Mon Paris. The song was also covered by Jack White for the twentieth anniversary covers album, and it also features in the film *The Great Gatsby*.

Tom Morello of Rage Against the Machine has chosen "Love is Blindness" as one of his favourite Edge moments.

Extras from the Era

"Alex Descends into Hell for a Bottle of Milk/Korova 1" was taken from Bono and The Edge's work on a Royal Shakespeare Company production of *A Clockwork Orange*. The performance debuted in London in 1990 and Bono and The Edge contributed to a pre-recorded score. The lyrics are in Latin.

"Lady with the Spinning Head" led U2 to multiple songs and featured as a B-side to "One." An extended remix was also issued. The lyrics touch on lady luck, who's spinning head sometimes means you win, and other times you lose. "Salomé" and "Where Did It All Go Wrong?" both appear on "Even Better Than the Real Thing." "Salomé" was a song worked on extensively in Berlin, but U2 could never get it to a finished state. The "Zooromancer Remix" of the song would be released as a promo to club DJs. "Where Did It All Go Wrong?" has elements of "Even Better than the Real Thing" and seems to have been a side path taken on the song.

Five additional original songs appeared on the twentieth anniversary collection. "Blow Your House Down" initially developed while recording *Rattle and Hum*. It was part of the Berlin sessions, and likely became "Lady with the Spinning Head" along the way. The version released includes new material recorded in 2011 to finish the song. New material was also recorded to finish "Heaven and Hell," another song from the Berlin sessions. "Oh Berlin" also has newly recorded vocals over an existing backing track, with Bono writing a love letter to Berlin, the city where the album was birthed. "Near the Island" is an instrumental piece from the 1991 sessions. The final track, "Down all the Days" is an early version of the song "Numb" which would be the first single released from U2's next album, *Zooropa*.

Zooropa
(1993)

Zooropa was recorded between March and May and released on July 5, 1993. U2 wanted to record an EP on a break from touring and ended up with a full album instead. The album was finished while U2 returned to touring, returning to Dublin to record between shows. Flood, Brian Eno, and The Edge acted as the producers for the album. Recording took place in The Factory, Windmill Lane Studios, and Westland Studios in Dublin.

Album designs were done by Steve Averill and Shaughn McGrath. The cover featured Cosmo, the *Achtung Baby* who had appeared on the CD label of that release. This time he is wearing a space helmet. U2 revisited the grid idea for the cover, using visuals from the ZooTV Tour. Over the images was a layer of purple text which listed song titles being worked on for the album, including three that would not appear until later, "Wake Up Dead Man," "Velvet Dress," and "Kiss Me Kill Me."

The album reached #1 in seventeen countries, including both the UK and the US. *Rolling Stone* listed the album at #61 on the 100 Best Albums of the Nineties. It was named Best Album and awarded for the best Album Sleeve at the *Hot Press* Music Awards. And the album won the Grammy Award in 1994 for Best Alternative Music Album.

The album was included in the 2011 collection celebrating the twentieth anniversary of *Achtung Baby*, but it was not remastered in that release. A proper remaster was issued on vinyl in 2018, including a remix of "Lemon" and "Numb" on the fourth side.

"ZOOROPA"
Lyrics: Bono
Music: U2
Producer: Flood/Eno/The Edge

"Zooropa" was developed as two songs, "Babel" included the whispered voices and advertising slogans, and "Zooropa" was the second portion of the song. Even when sent to reviewers the two were still separate songs. The second part had been captured by Joe O'Herlihy, U2's soundman, during a tour soundcheck. The song title is a mix of "Zoo" and "Europa." The lyric booklet features the lyrics of the song over the flags of many European nations.

The lyrics have Bono asking questions in English and French followed by advertising slogans from Audi ("Vorsprung Durch Technik" or "advancement through technology"), the US Army ("Be all that you can be"), the UK National Lottery ("Be a winner"), SlimFast ("Eat to get slimmer"), Persil laundry detergent ("A bluer kind of white"), United Airlines ("Fly the friendly skies"), Mild Green Fairy Liquid detergent ("We're mild and green and squeaky clean"), Zanussi appliances ("Through appliance of science"), Toshiba ("Better by design"). and Colgate toothpaste ("We've got that ring of confidence"). The album notes mention that the "Zooropa" opening is thanks to the advertising world.

Worried about the strangeness of "Numb," an edit of "Zooropa" was sent out in the US to stations unlikely to play "Numb" on air. "Zooropa" made it to #8 in the Album Rock Tracks chart and #13 on the Modern Rock Track chart in the US.

"Zooropa" ends with Bono talking about dreams, referencing "Acrobat" from the previous album.

"Babyface"
Lyrics: Bono
Music: U2
Producer: Flood/Eno/The Edge

During ZooTV, U2 had fallen in with a group of supermodels, including Christy Turlington, Helena Christensen, and Adam Clayton was engaged to Naomi Campbell. "Babyface" is inspired by models, but Bono takes it to a dark place, "there's a guy watching somebody on a TV, a personality, a celebrity he's obsessed with. It's about how people play with images, believing you know somebody through an image."[1]

The song has been played live just five times. The Edge said, "There's a real darkness about the song which a lot of reviewers who've talked about bubblegum pop, have missed, and the darkness of it seems to push the whole show so far into a pit that for me it never quite recovers till near the end of the show."[2]

"Numb"
Lyrics: The Edge
Music: U2
Producer: Flood/Eno/The Edge

"Numb" started out as "Down all the Days" during recording *Achtung Baby*. U2 tried several approaches including Bono reading his poem "In Cold Blood" over the backing music. The Edge finally took the song away and came up with the song we know today. It was the first single, and was so out there, U2 delivered copies of the album track on vinyl to radio stations without identifying U2 to see if stations would play the song. It was labeled "Produced by Fee Dognoodle" which can be unscrambled to "Flood, Edge, Eno."

The single was unconventional as well. Instead of the usual audio disc releases, the song was released exclusively as a videocassette. The only other high-profile video single at the time was Madonna's "Justify My Love." The single featured the video for "Numb," a video for a remix of "Numb" (remixed by Emergency Broadcast Network) and a video for "Love is Blindness." Australians also received live song clips to promote the Zoomerang Tour.

The video for "Numb," directed by Kevin Godley features The Edge sitting in front of the camera reciting the lyrics for the song. As he does so, random people walk through the video shoot and interact with him, blowing smoke in his face, kissing him, and tying him up with string. For a time, he is pushed out of the frame and Larry takes his place, with Adam in view behind. Bono, Paul McGuinness, and Edge's future wife, Morleigh Steinberg, are also among those in the video. The EBN Remix of "Numb" is "remixed" using loops of video footage, including clips of a first aid course, industrial machinery, and an army. These clips are intercut with video of The Edge singing in a darkened studio.

The song did not chart in the UK nor on the main US chart, but it made it to #39 on the Pop Songs Chart and #2 on the Alternative Charts in the US. It won the *Hot Press* Award for Best Video in 1994.

A new mix of the song was done by Mike Hedges for *The Best of 1990–2000* compilation. The Perfecto Mix, remixed by Paul Oakenfold featured on promotional releases, and included a short line from "In Cold Blood." An edit was also done for radio and distributed on promotional releases.

"LEMON"
Lyrics: Bono
Music: U2
Producer: Flood/Eno/The Edge

When Bono saw old video footage of his mother in a lemon-coloured dress, he was inspired to write "Lemon," one of the last songs completed for *Zooropa*. It was the second single, released in limited territories and formats. The single included different remixes of the title track, including remixes by Oakenfold, Steve Osbourne, and David Morales, as well as additional remixes on the promotional releases.

A video for "Lemon," directed by Mark Neale, was inspired by the work of Eadweard Muybridge, an early pioneer in motion picture projection and the study of animal locomotion. The video features U2 in their Zooropa Tour costumes, filmed in slow-motion against a grid in the same manner Muybridge filmed animals in motion. Bono appears as The Fly and Macphisto and a series of subtitles describe the action on screen. Alternate versions of the video included one with French-language subtitles, and a version without subtitles set to the "Bad Yard Club Edit."

"Lemon" has only been performed at ten shows in total on the ZooTV Tour, performed by Bono in his Macphisto persona, a devil-horned showman. The song has not been performed live since, but during The PopMart Tour, an instrumental version of Paul Oakenfold's "Perfecto Mix" was played over the PA as U2 moved into the giant mirror ball lemon for the encore. The video footage accompanying this portion of the show featured Australian performance artist Leigh Bowery.

Although "Lemon" did not chart in the UK, or the main USA charts, the song did make it to #1 in the *Billboard* Dance/Club Play chart and reached #3 on the Alternative Songs chart.

Tim Wheeler of rock band Ash has named "Lemon" as one of his favourite U2 songs.

"STAY (FARAWAY, SO CLOSE!)"

Lyrics: Bono
Music: U2
Producer: Flood/Eno/The Edge

"Stay (Faraway, So Close!)" initially developed late in the sessions for *Achtung Baby* under the name "Sinatra." Edge had been working on piano and was inspired by Sinatra. U2 reworked things while recording *Zooropa*. The Edge explains:

> It started out as a little acoustic guitar chord sequence that we worked up on the *Achtung Baby* record and Bono had this melody for it, but it never really took off. I rewrote the piece when we started on this record and demo-ed it with just guitar and drum machine. I was almost trying to write a Frank Sinatra song, it has some of the changes of chord and feel that I was going for, some of the discipline of that form of songwriting, which is very structured, very crafted. That's probably why it sounds the most like a formal U2 song.[3]

While U2 was recording, Wim Wenders approached them for a song for his next film, *Faraway, So Close!* U2 watched an early cut of the film and Bono found inspiration for lyrics in the film. The version appearing in the film was a longer track, with different drums and additional vocals. It was nominated for a Golden Globe Award for Best Original Song and found itself up against another Bono-penned track, "You Made Me the Thief of Your Heart" (performed by Sinéad O'Connor). Both tracks lost out to "Streets of Philadelphia" by Bruce Springsteen.

"Stay" was the third single, although in many countries, it was the first to see a traditional release. It was released as a double A-side with "I've Got You Under My Skin," Bono's duet with Frank Sinatra from Sinatra's *Duets* album. A video for "Stay (Faraway, So Close!)" was directed by Wim Wenders as a return favor for letting him use the song in his film. Set in Berlin, the clip stars German actress Meret Becker, whose stepfather, Otto Sander, was playing a lead role in Wenders' film. U2 appear in the video as guardian angels who watch over a young band. There are also several shots of U2 standing on the statue of Victoria, atop the Siegessäule monument in Berlin. A model of the statue was used for those scenes. Wenders had used the Siegessäule as a place where angels congregate in his 1987 film *Wings of Desire* (*Faraway, So Close!* is a sequel of sorts to that film). The final scene of the "Stay" video depicts Bono falling from the statue and landing in the street as he sings about an angel hitting the ground.

Bono rerecorded the song in 2001 with Craig Armstrong with a backing orchestra. A remix of the song by Underdog appeared on U2's first fan club release, *Melon*, and a second remix by Underdog featuring an alternate vocal singing different cities names featured on Underdog's *Greatest Bits Vol. 2* in 2012.

"Stay" reached #4 in the UK chart and hit #61 in the USA, the only song from *Zooropa* to chart on either.

Bono has named "Stay (Faraway, So Close!)" as his favourite U2 song in an interview in 2021.

"Daddy's Gonna Pay for Your Crashed Car"
Lyrics: Bono
Music: U2
Producer: Flood/Eno/The Edge

"Daddy's Gonna Pay for Your Crashed Car" is a song about addiction. Bono has said not necessarily about drugs, but anything we find ourselves addicted to. The song opens musical fanfare from "The Cliff" a song taken from an album of Lenin's favourite songs. The song also makes use of a sample of "The City Sleeps" throughout, a song by MC 900ft Jesus.

The song may have been looked at for a possible single, and stems were sent to DJs to produce remixes. Paul Oakenfold did one called The Perfecto Mix, often played in his sets, and used on his radio show. In 2020, we learned of another remix, this time by Butch Vig of Garbage. Vig programming his favourite songs on U2 X-Radio slipped in his own "Sunday Monday Tuesday Mix" of the song. Vig had been approached in the early '90s to mix songs from *Zooropa*, but this one, like Oakenfold's, remain unreleased.

"Some Days Are Better Than Others"
Lyrics: Bono
Music: U2
Producer: Flood/Eno/The Edge

Brian Eno did not work continuously with U2 in studio, he dropped in a few weeks at a time. Often, he worked in a second studio while U2 recorded in another. Eno pushed U2 to improvise, work on the music together, and then would help pull the pieces into a song. "Some Days Are Better Than Others" originated in a studio jam. The lyrics for "Some Days Are Better Than Others" were even tried out over another musical piece at one point, the music which became "Dirty Day."

In the book *U2 At the End of the World*, Bill Flanagan writes about Bono's inspiration for "Some Days Are Better Than Others":

> It's a pretty fair peek into Bono's current state of mind as he prowls around his house, trying not to trip over his children, his brain still filled with the smoke and mirrors of the Zoo TV tour. He is in that strange mental neighborhood where life on the road seems vibrant and natural and home life, real life, feels claustrophobic and flat.[4]

"Some Days Are Better Than Others" is the only song on *Zooropa* that has never been performed live. Only the one studio version exists.

"The First Time"
Lyrics: Bono
Music: U2
Producer: Flood/Eno/The Edge

While working on Zooropa, Bono had also been developing some songs for Al Green. One was called "Revolution of the Heart" and another was "The First Time." U2 decided to keep that one for themselves, and Al Green has never recorded a song penned by Bono. The song became a favourite of Bono's, "'The First Time' is a very special song. It just seemed right that in the middle of all the chaos and blinking lights of the futurescapes there would be a very simple, poetic moment."[5]

The Edge spoke about the song "It's almost like a film script starting out with characters and scenario and situation. We weren't quite sure until we were recording the song which way he was going to end the story."[6] The song did become a focal point of the film Bono scripted, *The Million Dollar Hotel*, released in 2000. Both the band version and an instrumental reprise recorded by Daniel Lanois with the Million Dollar Hotel Band are included in the soundtrack for the film.

Although the lyrics would sometimes be added to "Bad" in 1993, the song was not played in full until 2005's Vertigo Tour.

"DIRTY DAY"

Lyrics: Bono/The Edge
Music: U2
Producer: Flood/Eno/The Edge

"Dirty Day" was another song that came from improvisation in the studio. Bono took the title from his dad, "'It's a dirty day' was an expression my dad would use and there is a lot of him in there."[7] Other phrases in the song are also phrases used by Bono's dad.

One of the lines from the song is borrowed from a favourite author of Bono's, Charles Bukowski. Bukowski released a book of poems to his first love, Jane, titled *The Days Run Away Like Wild Horses Over the Hills*, published in 1969. Bono had met the author through Sean Penn. When *Zooropa* was being written, Bukowski was diagnosed with leukemia, and he passed away a few months after the release of the album. Bono said, "At the moment I'm toying with the idea of something that keeps flashing up in front of me when I hear the music, an image of a father giving surrealist advice to his son. I also see Charles Bukowski in my head and the kind of advice he gives, like 'Always give a false name!'"[8]

"Junk Day" and "Bitter Kiss" mixes were remixed by Butch Vig of Garbage in 1993. They were not used at the time, but both were included on the "Please" single in 1997.

The song debuted live in Australia and was played ten times during the ZooTV Tour. It was not heard again until it was resurrected for the final three shows on U2's 2018 tour where it was used to look back at the early years, and the influence their fathers had on U2.

THE WANDERER

Lyrics: Bono
Music: U2
Producer: Flood/Eno/The Edge

After playing a show with Kris Kristofferson in Dublin, Johnny Cash had Bono arrive backstage. He was invited to join U2 at Windmill Lane where U2 were working. Bono shared a song that had originated in the Berlin sessions, but had only recently been finished, called "The Preacher." According to the book *The Man Called Cash*, "they told him they were recording a track that was part of an experimental music project ... inspired by the Old Testament Book of

Ecclesiastes."[9] Johnny Cash did a vocal take for U2, but left Dublin assuming the track would never be used.

The track became the final song, and Bono is relegated to background vocals and Johnny Cash takes the lead. An alternate version of the song with an extra verse was given to Wim Wenders for use in the film *Faraway So Close*.

U2 performed the song in 2005 as part of a tribute concert to Johnny Cash. A second performance saw U2 in Nashville during the U2360° Tour, and it was played at the end of "I Still Haven't Found What I'm Looking For."

"The Wanderer" ends with an alarm noise, similar to those used by some radio stations to announce to the DJ that there is nothing playing. It is a jarring end to a lovely song.

Extras from the Era

Among the *Zooropa* singles there is one new U2 composition, a song called "Slow Dancing." Bono wrote the song for Willie Nelson to sing and while author Bill Flanagan was visiting in the studio, Flanagan asked if Bono could sing it. U2 recorded the song with Flood that evening, and released it on the "Stay (Faraway, So Close!)" single. In 1997, Willie Nelson travelled to Dublin, and would record the song with U2, and the song features in the documentary *Willie Nelson: Down Home* and on U2's single "If God Will Send His Angels."

Batman Forever director Joel Schumacher met with Bono about possibly appearing in the film as a villain, but in the end U2 only contributed a song, leftover from *Zooropa* sessions to the film. "Hold Me, Thrill Me, Kiss Me, Kill Me" can be seen written on the front cover of that album in the static, and was cut at the last minute. It was released June 5, 1995 as a single, and reached #2 in the UK, and #16 in the US, also hitting #1 on the Modern Rock Tracks charts. The video for the song, directed by Kevin Godley and Maurice Linnane was an animated one with Bono's characters of The Fly and MacPhisto running around Gotham, appearances by U2 in animated form, and even Batman and Robin making an appearance. The song was revived in 2018 for the intermission on U2's tour, this time performed by U2 with Gavin Friday on vocals, a long-time friend of U2, and included backing vocals by Regine Chassagne of Arcade Fire. U2 released this new version for Record Store Day's Black Friday event in 2018. The song was nominated for Best Rock Performance by a Duo or Group with Vocal and Best Rock Song at the 1996 Grammy Awards but did not win either. It was also nominated, but did not win, a Golden Globe.

9

Original Soundtracks 1
Passengers (1995)

Another side project that followed *Zooropa* was the Passengers album. U2 worked with Brian Eno as a fifth member and produced an entire album of soundtrack songs titled *Original Soundtracks 1*. Worried about the experimental nature of the album, the label convinced the band not to call it a U2 album, and the Passengers name was used instead. Some of the songs ended up in real films, but most were for imaginary films. The project started when Peter Greenaway, director of *The Pillow Book* approached U2 to work on some songs for the film, although no songs were used there. Brian Eno was one "passenger" on the album, but other guests included Japanese vocalist Holi, Pavarotti, and Howie B. The album was recorded at Westside Studios in London and Hanover Quay Studios in Dublin.

The cover art for the album was designed by Island Records' in-house designer Cally, and features artwork by Teodor Rotrekl. The sci-fi image is taken from the book *Šest dnů na Luně 1* (*Six Days on Luna 1*) by Ivo Štuka, published in 1963. In the UK the album charted at #12 and in the US it peaked at #76.

"United Colours," "Beach Sequence," "Always Forever Now," "Plot 180," "Theme from the Swan" and "Theme from Let's Go Native" are instrumental or feature minimal lyrics. In the case of "Always Forever Now" it is the title repeated throughout the song. Holi provides vocals on "Ito Okashi" in Japanese and shares vocals on "One Minute Warning" in Japanese. "Elvis Ate America" is Bono singing about Elvis Presley over a beat provided by Howie B. More traditional songs include "Slug," "A Different Kind of Blue," and "Corpse (These Chains Are Way Too Long)" with the last featuring The Edge on vocals.

In concert U2 have performed two songs from the album, "Miss Sarajevo" and "Your Blue Room." These are also the two songs that U2 promoted during the release of the album. "Miss Sarajevo" was released as a commercial single which reached #6 in the UK and did not chart in the US. The song was inspired by footage Bono saw of a beauty pageant being held in war-torn Sarajevo as people tried to find some sense of normality during wartime. The song featured Pavarotti on vocals. Videos for the song featured performance video from a concert in Italy where Bono and The Edge joined Brian Eno and Pavarotti for a performance, mixed with footage of the beauty pageant, and statistics about the war. The "Miss Sarajevo" single included an instrumental named "Viva Davidoff," a live version of "One" and a remix of "Zoo Station." "Your Blue Room" was also planned for a single release, but in the end, singles were sent out to radio only. The song features Adam Clayton on vocal at the end of the track. Two edits of "Miss Sarajevo" exist, the "Radio Edit" and the "Single Edit" and there is also an edited version of "Your Blue Room."

Songs from the Passengers project have ended up in the films *Heat, Ghost in the Shell,* and *Beyond the Clouds,* often with different edits of the song appearing. A cover of "Miss Sarajevo" by George Michael was released on his album *Songs from the Last Century.*

10

Pop
(1997)

Recording sessions for *Pop* started in mid-1995 with producer Nellee Hooper in France, Ireland, and the UK. In late 1995, U2 moved to Hanover Quay in Dublin, where the remainder of the work was completed with Flood, Howie B, and Steve Osbourne listed as producers on Pop. Some recording was also completed at South Beach Studios in Miami as well as Windmill Lane and at The Works in Dublin.

Originally announced for an October 14, 1996 release, *Pop* was delayed due to troubles finishing the songs. U2 had been so confident in that release date they booked the PopMart Tour to start in April 1997. The October date was missed, and U2 pushed *Pop* back to March 3, 1997, and work on completion of the album cut in on the preparation time normally spent on tour preparation.

Pop got its name from Larry Mullen, "I just said to the guys 'Look *Pop* looks great on T-shirts, so why don't we call the album *Pop*?'"[1] The art was directed by Steve Averill and Shaughn McGrath.

Pop had a strong debut, reaching #1 in twenty-nine countries, including both the UK and US. *Pop* did receive mixed reviews, and U2 themselves showed some unhappiness with the album as they went back and re-recorded or remixed several of the songs for singles, including "Discothèque," "Please," and "Last Night on Earth" and further songs were changed for use on *The Best of 1990–2000* compilation. It has been listed at #35 in *Hot Press*' 100 Greatest Irish Albums of All Times in 2005 and did win *Hot Press* Awards in 1998 for Best Irish Album and Best Album Sleeve. *Pop* was nominated but did not win Best Rock Album at the 1998 Grammy Awards.

A remastered version directed by The Edge was released on iTunes in 2017 and followed on vinyl in 2018.

"DISCOTHÈQUE"
Lyrics: Bono/Edge
Music: U2
Producer: Flood

Bono says "Discothèque" is "an earnest little riddle about love."[2] Edge shared U2 had decided to abandon what U2 had sounded like before and focus on new forms of making music.[3] The song was one of the last finished, with Bono deciding last minute the song needed a new intro even though *Pop* was being mastered. Howie B jumped in and produced a new intro on the spot. The original intro can be heard on the single. Flood told *Propaganda*, "Howie had this mad techno-groove. It was right at the end of the day. Edge picked up the bass and just started playing. Bono picked up the mike and started jamming melodies over the top. The piece was about 15 minutes long. Larry heard it and said, 'OK, I could put this sort of drums on it.'"[4] The *Pop* album was the first time U2 widely used samples in their work. "Discothèque" included a credited sample of the song "Freeform" (1995) by Fane, borrowing a drum loop from the song.

"Discothèque" brought U2's first internet leak. A snippet of the song included on a press kit appeared on the internet in October 1996. The full song also leaked in advance of the radio debut, causing U2 to move the radio release ahead.

An edit of the song was sent to radio to promote the song. The single featured mixes of "Discothèque" by David Holmes, David Morales, Howie B, and Steve Osbourne. Three sizes of disco balls were also sent out for promotion of the song.

"Discothèque" reached #10 in the US charts, as well as charting on the Alternative Songs (#1) and the Dance/Club Play Songs (#1) charts. It also reached #1 in the UK charts.

A video filmed by Stéphane Sednaoui featured U2 performing the song in a giant mirror ball built at Pinewood Studios in London. U2 were dressed in outrageous costumes reminiscent of The Village People. Asked how U2 chose their costumes The Edge shared "I think my moustache was the thing that got me in the leather man gear" while Adam revealed, "There was a big fight over who was going to be the sailor but eventually I won."[5, 6] Addressing rumours that he was uncomfortable with the video itself, Larry Mullen explained, "People thought I was a little bit embarrassed or shy. In actual fact it was after seeing Edge in the get up I was like shocked. I couldn't get over it at all. I'm still not over it."[7] Additional videos were developed for David Morales and Hexidecimal Mix remixes of the song. These used footage from the Sednaoui video, mixed with computer graphics, wireframe treatments, and other fun elements.

U2 included "Discothèque" on *The Best of 1990–2000* but instead of using one of the original mixes of the song, producer Mike Hedges compiled a new mix.

"DO YOU FEEL LOVED"
Lyrics: Bono/Edge
Music: U2
Producer: Osbourne/Flood

In 1996, Naked Funk released their album *Valium* on Howie B's Pussyfoot Records. Howie B was a fan of the song "Alien Groove Sensation" and played the song for U2. U2 started to riff over the song, and it became "Do You Feel Loved." Howie had met U2 in London, and U2 had fallen in love with him. They worked with him as part of the Passengers product, he was present throughout the recording of *Pop*, and he joined U2 on the PopMart Tour, spinning records before U2 took the stage. The Naked Funk track is credited as inspiration for the song, and not as a sample, as U2 rerecorded the portions they used. Bono said, "We wanted to make a sexy, groovy song and we nearly did!"[8]

Bono suggested the song was meant to be sung in front of 50,000 people in a stadium, and U2 worked on the song for the PopMart Tour but never got it to a place where they were happy with the performances. After being played only six times U2 abandoned further attempts.

"MOFO"

Lyrics: Bono/Edge
Music: U2
Producer: Flood

Bono has spoken about the song as containing his whole life in just a few lines, sharing, "The song 'Mofo' was first called 'The Return of The Fly', like a B-movie and then it became the heaviest song maybe we ever written."[9] The song discusses his mother, the loss he feels, all the way to talking about his children. Discussing the lyric about a black hole, Bono says:

> Everyone's got one. Some are blacker and wider than others. It goes right back to the blues. It's what first makes you want to shout at God, when you've been abandoned, or someone's been taken away from you. And I don't think you ever fill it, not completely. You can fill it up with time, by living a full life, but, if you're silent enough, you can still hear the hissing.[10]

"Mofo" was released simultaneously with the "If God Will Send His Angels" single as the fifth singles released from *Pop*. Several remixes of "Mofo" were released including mixes by Matthew Roberts, Roni Size and Leo Pearson. A video for "Mofo" directed by Maurice Linnane was set to the "Phunk Phorce Mix" and was released in January 1997 to coincide with the launch of the PopMart Tour in Australia. The video is made up of tour clips, including a pregnant Morleigh Steinberg belly dancing in Oslo for Edge's birthday.

Actor Woody Harrelson has named "Mofo" as his favourite song on *Pop*, which he calls his favourite U2 release. Bono has also named the song as one of his favourites on *Pop*, telling the BBC:

I was in the Kitchen, which is a club here in Dublin, Propellerheads were playing and it was a big deal for me to hear it on … I don't know how somebody got a tune before they should have, it just came on and surprised me. "Mofo." That blew me away. I like that. It's pretty full on alright. I feel like it's my whole life in that tune. That's pretty sad, when your whole life can be summed up in one tune.[11]

"IF GOD WILL SEND HIS ANGELS"
Lyrics: Bono/Edge
Music: U2
Producer: Flood/Howie B

Bono wrote the song about a guy giving his girlfriend a hard time looking for answers. Bono described the song: "Each song is its own little world, that's what this record is going to be like, I think. 'If God Will Send his Angels' is like a Temptations song—something like that would not normally find itself on the same record as a hardcore rocking song like 'Last Night on Earth'."[12] He would also say of the song, "It's like science fiction gospel. Edge is calling it country hip-hop."[13]

The song developed during the *Zooropa* sessions. It was the fifth single, released concurrently with "Mofo." Like two previous singles, "If God Will Send His Angels" was rerecorded and released in a "single version" that differed substantially from that found on *Pop*.

The song was a strange choice for a single as the song had long since been dropped from performances. The lyrical references to Christmas may have motivated U2 to release the song for the Christmas season, with Bono saying: "It is a beautiful tune. It is one of my favourites on the record. I think it should really spoil Christmas day next year for a lot of people.… I think there's hope in the song, but it looks a little bleak."[14] In 1997, the release was accompanied by a promotional advent calendar, and in 2021, the song was included in a streaming compilation of U2 Christmas songs.

A video filmed by Phil Joanou was shot in a diner in Detroit, depicting Bono sitting at a table, while people come in and out of the diner including the band. Bono was filmed at a low framerate, and the footage was later sped up.

The single version also features in the film *City of Angels*, a remake of a Wim Wenders film, *Wings of Desire*. An alternate edit of the video interspersed scenes from the film with Joanou's original footage.

"STARING AT THE SUN"
Lyrics: Bono/Edge
Music: U2
Producer: Flood
Additional: Osbourne/Hooper

"Staring at the Sun" was partially inspired by Irish band Something Happens. That group's second album was called *Stuck Together with God's Glue*, a phrase Bono borrowed for the lyrics here. In *U2 by U2* Bono says "I think it nails a certain mood, where you actually don't want to know the truth because lies are more comforting."[15]

The song was the second single, and unlike most of the singles from *Pop*, there was not a different version of the track on the single. The single featured several remixes by Butch Vig (of Garbage) and Danny Saber. The single reached #26 on the Hot 100 chart in the US, and #1 on the Alternative Songs chart. In the UK, the single reached #3. A kaleidoscope was distributed to promote the song.

A video directed by Jake Scott was filmed in New York, featuring U2 in darkness with a series of light effects around them to create atmosphere. A second video directed by Morleigh Steinberg included footage of U2 filmed around Miami as photo shoots for the *Pop* album were done.

The song was one of the songs which caused U2 trouble in concert, and eventually they would abandon a full band performance, favouring a stripped back acoustic version.

"Staring at the Sun" was remixed by Mike Hedges for *The Best of 1990–2000* compilation. The production team known as Brothers in Rhythm also worked on two remixes of the song releasing them as a 12-inch promo used as promotion for that compilation.

"Last Night on Earth"
Lyrics: Bono and Edge
Music: U2
Producer: Flood

"Last Night on Earth" was developed during *Zooropa* recording sessions. It was revisited during sessions for *Pop* and was one of the last songs U2 worked on. With the deadline to finish *Pop* looming, U2 rushed to finish it. They were unhappy with the result and the roughness of Bono's voice.

Bono remembers the recording of the song:

It was four o'clock in the morning of the last night in the studio. We had people mixing who hadn't been in bed for a week. Paul was waiting to take the tapes to New York to master the record. I started singing the line: "You've got to give it away." Don't turn it into work was the message. Which was exactly what we were doing. We were supposed to be making an uplifting expression of what happens when rock 'n' roll meets club culture. Instead, it felt like a load of men on an oil rig in the middle of the North Sea.[16]

Unhappy with the song, U2 booked time at Signature Sound in San Diego once the tour was underway. They rerecorded the track and used a new recording for the single. The song was the third released from *Pop*. On the single was an instrumental remix of "Last Night on Earth." A stress ball painted to look like a globe was issued to promote the song.

The song featured a sample from "Trayra Boia" by the group Codona from their 1982 album *Codona 3*. It is comprised primarily of layers of conversational voices, including a falsetto.

A video filmed by Richie Smyth in Kansas City, shut down sections of two interstate highways. The clip depicted an apocalyptic future filled with abandoned cars, people walking around like zombies with slime dripping from their hands, a spilled truck of lemons, and U2 in a retro car with a young female hitchhiker. They eventually assist the military in identifying the source of a mysterious glowing light—only to discover that the source is author William S. Burroughs. The young girl is played by Sophie Dahl, granddaughter of writer Roald Dahl and actress Patricia Neal.

"Gone"
Lyrics: Bono/Edge
Music: U2
Producer: Flood

Bono spoke about "Gone":

> Obviously in this song I am talking about the past. You know people complain about being rock & roll-stars, you hear them all the time these spoiled popstars, how hard it is. From the moment Larry asked me to be in this band it's just been a big adventure and when "Gone" was written I felt like it was almost the last song ever for us. But that was what I was feeling that day. What I wanted to say, it was fantastic, I loved all of this, even the bullshit, I enjoyed it all, so I could lose that too.[17]

During the PopMart Tour "Gone" was often dedicated to Michael Hutchence, lead singer of INXS and close friend to Bono, who had died during while U2 were on tour.

Although the song was not released as a single, U2 did include it on *The Best of 1990–2000* but a reworked version done with producer Mike Hedges.

"Miami"
Lyrics: Bono/Edge
Music: U2
Producer: Howie B/Flood
Original: Hooper

The song was one of the latter songs completed. Howie B told *Hot Press* he had been arguing with Bono up to the end of the sessions about the lyrics and the final verse was only written and recorded while the final mix was being done.[18]

Adam discussed heading to Miami for recording sessions, "We'd been in the studio for a while, slugging it out with the direction of the record. And it's a very nice place to be stuck for six months or so—but I think at that stage we all needed a bit of fresh air. So, we went to Miami and we had a very good time!"[19] U2 had also looked at Cuba as an option when looking for a warmer climate to do some work.

The song was performed each night on the first two legs of the PopMart Tour, but made only two appearances on the third leg, one being in Miami itself.

"THE PLAYBOY MANSION"
Lyrics: Bono/Edge
Music: U2
Producer: Flood/Howie B

When asked on the BBC what his favourite track on the new album was, Larry Mullen was quick to mention this song, "I haven't listened to the album as much. When you finish something like this, it's like being in the trenches, you really don't feel ready to take it all in. The one track I always liked, even from its earliest stage was 'Playboy Mansion'. And even though I haven't listened to it for a while I love the lyric. That's my fave!"[20] Bono calls the song "a hymn to trash."[21]

The song is structured around an inspiration from another song, "You Showed Me" by The Turtles. Howie B explains, "It was a Turtles song which I played them, and U2 were inspired by that. One of the guitar riffs Edge plays on 'The Playboy Mansion' is inspired by that song, but we didn't actually use any samples on it. Edge played the riff and made it his own, but we thought we'd better respect the fact that we had been inspired by that song; that's why there's the credit."[22]

While a favourite song of Larry Mullen, the song is the only song from *Pop* never performed in concert although Bono will sometimes work the lyrics into other songs.

"IF YOU WEAR THAT VELVET DRESS"
Lyrics: Bono/Edge
Music: U2
Producer: Flood
Original: Hooper

"If You Wear That Velvet Dress" was a leftover from the *Zooropa* sessions. It is one of the songs that can be seen written on the cover of that album. Bono's been quiet about the song but has said, "'If You Wear That Velvet Dress'—I don't want to talk about that song too much, but let's just say it's haunted. It's all tangled up in ultraviolet."[23]

Like many of the other songs on *Pop*, Bono did rerecord the song, but this time it was not with U2. In 2002, he recorded the song with Jools Holland and his Rhythm and Blues Orchestra. The song is reimagined with an orchestra of strings backing Bono's vocal.

"PLEASE"
Lyrics: Bono/Edge
Music: U2
Producer: Flood/Howie B

Bono names "Please" as a favourite. "My other favourite tune at the moment is 'Please' I think that's going to be extraordinary when we take it out live."[24] He claims to have sung the original album version in only one take. The song deals with the conflict in Northern Ireland. Bono in *U2 by U2* talks about the song, "It is a song about terror, really. Are there ever any excuses for it? It was the Docklands bombing in London that it referred to and the breakdown of peace talks in Northern Ireland but after 9/11 it became impossible to sing."[25]

"Please" was the fourth single released. A second release featuring the song, the "PopHeart EP, featured live performances. The cover of "Please" featured four men with tinted faces: Gerry Adams, leader of Ireland's Sinn Féin party (top left); David Trimble, of the Ulster Unionist Party (top right); Ian Paisley, leader of the Democratic Unionist Party (bottom right); and John Hume, leader of the Social Democratic and Labour Party (bottom left). All four were involved in the contentious Northern Ireland peace process, which was itself part of the inspiration for the song. Bono even managed to bring Trimble and Hume on stage in Belfast during a performance to shake hands.

The single featured a newly recorded version of "Please." U2 were unhappy with the version on *Pop*, feeling that it was unfinished. U2 recorded this new version at Wisseloord Studios in Hilversum, the Netherlands, while on the PopMart Tour.

A video by Anton Corbijn features a village with people on their knees, mixed with clips of Bono singing. A young girl and an older man are the focus of the clip. The man appears to be homeless with a sign around his neck that reads "Please." When the song kicks into high gear, the footage of Bono becomes coloured, and most of the characters rise from their knees while the older man falls to the ground. A second video, directed by Maurice Linnane features audio recorded at the Helsinki PopMart show, and video footage from various concerts. The live video footage is interspersed with images of political murals in Northern Ireland.

The single charted in the USA at #31 on the Alternative Songs chart and #7 on the UK Charts.

Irish radio personality and DJ, Dave Fanning names "Please" his favourite from *Pop*.[26]

"Wake Up Dead Man"
Lyrics: Bono/Edge
Music: U2
Producer: Flood
Original: Hooper

Some of the songs on *Pop* came quickly, but this one did not. As early as the *Achtung Baby* sessions in Berlin, Bono was working on a song called "Wake Up Dead Man" and it went through several iterations. It nearly made it onto *Zooropa* and if you look closely, you can find it mentioned in the cover artwork. The song dates to at least 1986, when Bono mentioned the title in interviews while working on *The Joshua Tree*. The song comes from a lyric idea by The Edge. Speaking of the version worked out for *Zooropa*, Bono said, "It wasn't right. We had a very gothic version of it, but as you should know if you don't already, Gothic is against the law, it's the flared trousers of the 80s and 90s, and it should be avoided at all times. I didn't like the version we had back then. This is as light as you can be with a song as heavy with that."[27]

The song itself is an angry conversation. "I've been boring people about religion for years. It's a fairly pissed off tune. I guess it's picking up on the way a lot of people feel outside. If there is a God 'What the fuck? Why are things the way they are?" Bono relates.[28] The song does use profanity, a rarity on U2 albums, which resulted in an edited version of the song in Malaysia.

The song includes a sample of "Besrodna Nevesta" by Le Mystere Des Voix Bulgares. It is layered in behind the voices in the mix.

Bono said, "We didn't really want to end with that, but you can't help it. It's an ending song."[29]

Extras from the Era

"Holy Joe" was played at the press conference where U2 announced the PopMart Tour in the lingerie section of a K-Mart in Manhattan. It featured as a B-side on the "Discothèque" single. Two versions were released, the "Guilty Mix" and the "Garage Mix."

"North and South of the River" was written by Bono and The Edge with Irish folk singer Christy Moore. It was released as a single by the three of them in 1995, reaching #17 on the Irish charts. In the liner notes to his album *On the Road*, Christy Moore reflects, "I enjoyed working with Bono and The Edge 20 years ago. It was a creative experience that I still cherish ... and I still love singing this song."[30] U2 recorded the song themselves as a B-side for "Staring at the Sun."

"I'm Not Your Baby" was recorded by U2 with Sinéad O'Connor for the Wim Wenders film *The End of Violence* released in September 1997. The song was recorded at the same sessions where the band re-recorded "Last Night on Earth" and vocals are shared between Bono and Sinéad. An instrumental version of the song was released on the "Please" single, and an alternate mix of the song with vocals featured on a German promotional single.

"Two Shots of Happy One Shot of Sad" first appeared as the B-side to "If God Will Send His Angels" and is a song that Bono and The Edge wrote for Frank Sinatra to sing, but Sinatra never recorded it before his death. In 2004, Nancy Sinatra recorded the song, with Larry Mullen and Adam Clayton filling out her rhythm section. Bono performed the song with The Imposters in 2009 at an appearance on *Spectacle: Elvis Costello.*

All That You Can't Leave Behind (2000)

All That You Can't Leave Behind was released on October 30, 2000. The album takes its name from a lyric from "Walk On." Album recording included the bands houses in the South of France, and several studios in Dublin including Hanover Quay, Windmill Lane, Westland, and Totally Wired Studios. The primary producers were longtime collaborators Brian Eno and Daniel Lanois. Additional production on the album was done by Steve Lillywhite, Mike Hedges, Richard Stannard, and Julian Gallagher. Recording started in late 1998 and continued through until 2000. There was a break in the sessions where Bono worked with Lanois on the *Million Dollar Hotel* soundtrack. The album was publicized as a return to U2's earlier sound.

The cover features the band photographed at Charles de Gaulle airport in Paris. The black and white photography was a choice by designers Shaughn McGrath and Steve Averill to contrast with the artwork from the nineties. The gate label "F21-36" has been edited and has been replaced with "J33-3" a reference to the bible verse Jeremiah 33:3, "Call unto me and I will answer thee great and mighty things which thou knowest not."

The album reached #1 in thirty-two different countries, including the US *Billboard* Top 200 and the UK Charts. The album won "Best Rock Album" at the 2002 Grammy Awards. It is the only album to have two singles win "Record of the Year" at the Grammy Awards in consecutive years. The album is listed in Robert Dimery's *1001 Albums You Must Hear Before You Die* book. It won Best Album and Best Rock Album at the Meteor Awards and was given the *Hot Press* Award for Best Irish Rock Album. *Rolling Stone* has also listed the album in the list of 500 Albums (#139 in 2003 and #280 in 2012) as well as #13 at their list of Best Albums of the Decade (2010).

A remastered version was issued at iTunes in 2017, directed by The Edge. In 2018, this version was also released on black vinyl. In 2020, a twentieth anniversary edition of the album was released, expanded to include "The Ground Beneath

Her Feet" but using the same 2017 remaster otherwise. The boxed set included rarities, B-sides, and a full Elevation show from Boston in audio formats. In 2022, a special pressing of the album was done to celebrate the thirtieth anniversary of Interscope Records. Just 100 copies were pressed featuring a painting by John Currin, *Newspaper Couple*, on the cover.

"Beautiful Day"
Lyrics: Bono
Music: U2
Producer: Lanois/Eno
Additional: Lillywhite

"Beautiful Day" was released as the first single but at one-point U2 considered leaving it off the album, "We had this song called 'Beautiful Day' a surf-punk song, and now it's a New Age hymn. Maybe it's on the record—it wasn't last week." said Bono while U2 were still recording.[1] The Edge explained the indecision, "it came down to, is it really good or is it a rehash? If it's good and we're just chucking it out because it reminds us of U2, then that's actually not a very good reason to throw it out."[2] Edge was happy to leave the song intact, stating, "Beautiful Day it's the best song on the record, I think. It's like rock n roll, it's a band in full flight."[3]

"Beautiful Day" developed from a song called "Always," you hear Edge singing the title under Bono's vocal. "Always" was released with "Beautiful Day." Bono was inspired to write the lyrics from his experiences with Jubilee 2000 urging politicians to drop world debt. The song is about someone who has lost everything but finds joy in what they have. Some of the lyrics have Bono thinking about Earth from above, an idea revisited during the U2360° Tour, when it was introduced by astronauts looking down from the International Space Station.

Jonas Åkerlund filmed a video at Charles de Gaulle Airport, Paris. Footage of U2 walking around the airport was interspersed with shots of them performing on carpets on the airport runway while jets take off overhead. A second video directed by Joe Edwards, shows U2 recording the album in-studio, mixed with vacation footage from the south of France.

Remixes of the song by David Holmes, Paul Oakenfold, and Quincey & Sonance were included on the single. Oakenfold would release a new remix in 2004. In 2019, as U2 were heading to India for the first time, they asked Indian DJs to remix songs for an EP, and Amaal Mallik remixed "Beautiful Day" for "The Eternal Remixes."

The song reached #1 in the UK, a surprise to many expecting Kylie Minogue and Robbie Williams to take the top spot. In the US, "Beautiful Day" reached #21 on the Hot 100, and charted for Adult Pop Songs (#4), Alternative Songs (#5), Pop Songs (#19), and the Dance/Club Play (#1). The song was nominated for Video of the Year at the MTV Video Music Awards. It was listed in *Rolling Stone*'s "Greatest Songs of All Time" at #345 in 2010. "Beautiful Day" won three Grammy Awards at the 2001 ceremony, Song of the Year, Record of the Year, and Best Rock Performance by a Duo or Group with Vocal. The song was U2's fourth most streamed song at the end of 2021 on Spotify.

"Beautiful Day" was used in coverage of the 2000 Olympics in Sydney Australia and it was theme music for *The Premiership*, a weekly broadcast of English Premier League football on ITV. In 2020, during the pandemic, with many graduation ceremonies cancelled, YouTube hosted "Dear Class of 2020" a virtual graduation celebration. Bono spoke at the event, and introduced a cover of "Beautiful Day" lead by Finneas, and including artists like Chris Martin of Coldplay, Camila Cabello, and Ty Dolla $ign.

Michael Stipe of R.E.M. commented on "Beautiful Day," "I love that song. I wish I'd written it, and they know that I'd wish I'd written it. It makes me dance. It makes me angry that I didn't write it."[4]

"STUCK IN A MOMENT YOU CAN'T GET OUT OF"
Lyrics: Bono/Edge
Music: U2
Producer: Lanois/Eno

"Stuck in a Moment You Can't Get Out Of" was developed by The Edge during the PopMart Tour, "it started out as just an idea I had for a kind of gospel direction for something. Bono kicked it in a very different direction."[5] One version of the song recorded, but never released, included vocals by Mick Jagger and his daughter Elizabeth.

Bono said little about the origins of the song until U2 did an appearance at Irving Plaza, "This is a song about friendship. It's for a good friend, Michael Hutchence."[6] Bono would later tell *Rolling Stone*:

> I think other people who have lost a mate to suicide will tell you the same thing— the overpowering guilt that you weren't there for that person. As anyone around here will tell you, friendship is a thing that I hold very sacred.... So I just remember feeling this overpowering sense of guilt. And anger. And annoyance. That song is an argument. It's a row between mates. You're kind of trying to slap somebody around the face, trying to wake them out of an idea. In my case it's a row I didn't have when he was alive.[7]

"Stuck in a Moment" was the second single everywhere except North America, where "Walk On" was used instead. In North America, it was the fourth single instead, with a shorter "radio edit" and an "acoustic version" released. The song reached #2 in the UK charts and it reached #52 in the USA. A cassette single issued in the UK was the last cassette single released by U2. A special CD single was released in a cloth sleeve featuring live songs from a promotional appearance in Paris.

A video directed by Kevin Godley, filmed in Los Angeles, featured Bono being repeatedly thrown out of a moving vehicle and attempting to get up. The band tries to cross a busy highway to reach him, and at the end, The Edge gives him a hand to get up. A second video, directed by Joe Edwards, features footage of U2 recording at Hanover Quay in Dublin, at photo shoots for the album and relaxing in the South of France. A third video, directed by Joseph Kahn, features a recreation of an American football game, complete with a guest appearance by American football analyst John Madden. The game is between "The Flys" and "The Lemons" at "The Unforgettable Fire Dome" and a rookie player, named Paul Hewson, misses the final kick, and replays the game in his mind over and over.

Adam Clayton discussed the song in 2021:

> ... the idea behind it was to try and address how we felt about losing Michael Hutchence at the time and he was our generation. He was our brother and our competitor in many ways. We both had bands with names made up of letters, they were from Australia, we were from Ireland, you know, there was so many connections. And we used to spend what we call our summer holidays in the south of France with Michael.[8]

The song was nominated for Song of the Year and Best Pop Performance by a Duo or Group with Vocal at the 2002 Grammy Awards but only won the latter category. The song was U2's tenth most streamed song at the end of 2021 on Spotify.

In 2021, a version of "Stuck" recorded by actress Scarlett Johansson was featured in the film *Sing 2*. The song is used in a scene where Scarlett's character Ash attempts to convince Bono's character Clay to leave his self-imposed seclusion.

"ELEVATION"
Lyrics: Bono
Music: U2
Producer: Lanois/Eno

"Elevation" is a lighter song after a somber note. Bono told *Rolling Stone*, "It's a tune called 'Elevation' It's in its raw form. I think it's gonna go off for us. It's got a really spongy sound. We've found that when you're men, the slower tempos can be funky."[9] The song was the third single from the album, and featured in a summer blockbuster, *Lara Croft: Tomb Raider*, the fourteenth biggest film in the USA in 2001.

"Elevation" was remixed by Chris Vrenna for the single and it was this "Tomb Raider Mix" used in the film. Remixes by Paul Van Dyk, Quincey and Sonance, Jon Carter, Richard Stannard, and Julian Gallagher, and Leo Pearson were done for the single. The remix by Pearson, "The Influx Mix" was used nightly to open the Elevation Tour. U2 also released their first DVD single to accompany the song.

A special effects-filled video was directed by Joseph Kahn. U2 were fighting evil doppelgangers, and The Edge was digitally inserted into footage from *Lara Croft: Tomb Raider* interacting with Angelina Jolie. The video features giraffes, fire engines, explosions, Larry Mullen on a motorcycle, and flying elephants!

The song reached #3 in the UK. Although it missed charting on the main *Billboard* chart, it charted on the Alternative Charts (#8) and the Dance/Club Play Songs (#32). The song won Best Rock Performance by a Duo or Group at the 2002 Grammy Awards and "Elevation" was nominated for Best Rock Song but did not win the award. It was nominated for "Best Video from a Film" and "Best Group Video" at the MTV Video Music Awards.

"WALK ON"
Lyrics: Bono
Music: U2
Producer: Lanois/Eno
Additional: Lillywhite

"Walk On" is dedicated to Aung San Suu Kyi, a politician from Burma. She won the election to lead the country in 1990, but the military refused to hand over power, placing her under house arrest for fifteen years. *Time* magazine named her a "child of Ghandi," she won a Nobel Peace Prize. In 2000, she and U2 were awarded the Freedom of the City of Dublin. At the ceremony, U2 met with Suu Kyi's son who had accepted the award on her behalf.

Bono used her story to inspire lyrics for "Walk On," looking at the separation from her family. Bono said, "her story is interesting, and I found it inspirational for the song, because it is about someone who left a very comfortable life in Oxford in England—left her family, left her sons, left her husband—and went back to Burma to face imprisonment, assassination."[10]

U2 released the song as the second single in North America, with an "edit" of the song sent to radio. The rest of the world saw "Walk On" released as the fourth single from the album. The later single release saw new mixes, the "single version" and "video version" of the song. The single version was reworked by Nigel Godrich. The video version reworked by Steve Lillywhite. Additional mixes included a "Remix" sent to radio with slightly tweaked instrumental levels, and a unique mix by Mike Hedges called the "Hallelujah Mix," issued after U2 had won several Grammys in 2002. An acoustic version of the song was used in the film *Burma Soldier*, and a remix of the song by Wyclef Jean was released for a twentieth anniversary boxed set.

"Walk On" reached #5 in the UK. It did not chart in the US. The song won Record of the Year in 2002 at the Grammy Awards, and while nominated for Best Rock Song and Best Rock Performance by a Duo or Group with Vocal it did not win either award. The version nominated in 2002 was from the *America: A Tribute to Heroes* album, recorded with Dave Stewart, Natalie Imbruglia, Morleigh Steinberg and Medhi Parisot for a telethon in the wake of the September 11 attacks.

A video directed by Liz Friedlander showed U2 performing in London, intercut with people running through the streets, being bullied, and later escaping their situations and tearing at their clothing. A second video, directed by Jonas Åkerlund, was filmed in Rio de Janeiro, Brazil. The band interacts with fans, walk through Rio, play soccer on the beach, and perform the song at Globo studios. A third video produced by MTV in the wake of the September 11 attacks in New York. It featured U2's music over scenes of the destruction and rescue teams in action.

In recent years, Aung San Suu Kyi returned to lead Burma and has been criticized for her inaction in response to the genocide of the Rohingya people by her government. U2 rescinded the dedication to Suu Kyi from the 2020 pressings of the album. A new dedication has been added to the video for "Walk On," "This song is dedicated to the Rohingya people whose human rights have been so persistently and brutally denied."

In 2022, as part of the Stand Up for Ukraine campaign, Bono and The Edge shared an acoustic version of "Walk On" with lyrics updated to address the war between Russia and Ukraine. Bono and The Edge would perform the song with others in a subway station in Kyiv during the Russian invasion.

Adam Clayton looking back on the song in 2020 said, "when I go back to it now, I go, 'That is world class. So that's up there with anybody else's songs.'"[11]

"KITE"

Lyrics: Bono/Edge
Music: U2
Producer: Lanois/Eno

"Kite" is a letter written by Bono to his kids, realizing some day they would grow up and have their own lives. But The Edge could see it was something more. Bono's father was dying of cancer and Edge could see that there was another goodbye in the lyrics, and that Bono was writing about father and a son. "I hadn't been around for a while and was determined to do the proper Dad thing. I took the kids to Killiney Hill in Dublin County to fly a kite. Up it went and immediately down

it came and smashed to smithereens. The kids just looked at me: 'Come on, Dad, let's go and play some video games.' How cruel is that?"[12]

The song developed quickly, and Bono claims it was done in a single take, "there's no overdubs on it. It is just kind of a string/loop that Edge put together. I think it is an extraordinary bass part, sort of almost dub bass part."[13]

A particularly beautiful version of the song captured live in Sydney appeared on the "Window in the Skies" single, complete with didgeridoo courtesy of Tim Moriarty. Although never released as a single, the live version recorded in Boston was released to some music stations to promote the release of the Live from Boston video.

"IN A LITTLE WHILE"
Lyrics: Bono
Music: U2
Producer: Eno/Lanois
Additional: Stannard/Gallagher

"In a Little While" was recorded after Bono had spent a late-night partying. "It was performed after a very heavy night out on the town. So, you can actually hear in his voice the rasp of a late night with much revelry and high spirits. I think it's quite an interesting marriage of something quite traditional and something quite new."[14] The lyrics include references to Bono's wife Ali and how he was teased he was robbing the cradle when she was younger. The song also talks about humanity looking to space, other scientific achievements, and realizing science would not save humanity.

The space connection came to life on the U2360° Tour. Bono would often communicate with the astronauts on the International Space Station during the tour, and at time lyrics were read by astronauts on the station. In the concert filmed at the Rose Bowl, Belgium astronaut Frank DeWinne reads the lyrics. "In a Little While" was covered by William Shatner and Lyle Lovett for an album of "space songs" that the former Captain Kirk actor had put together.

A remix titled the "N.O.W. Remix" was released on *Café del Mar: The Best of Compiled* and later was issued on the twentieth anniversary collection of the album.

"In a Little While" was a favorite of Joey Ramone and was the last song he heard before his death according to his family.

"WILD HONEY"
Lyrics: Bono
Music: U2
Producer: Eno/Lanois

According to the *Irish Times*, "Wild Honey" was almost issued as the second single from the album.[15] Like "Elevation" the song is a lighter tune in an album full of heavier songs. Looking back twenty years later, The Edge said "We almost didn't put it on the album because it sounded so bright, so shiny, so sweet. But what it has, is a kind of innocence and a kind of naiveté, which is very important when it's followed by 'Peace on Earth', which is probably one of the bleakest songs that U2 have ever written."[16]

The song came so easy to U2 they thought they should leave it, but "everyone that heard it thought it was just the best thing. So, we kind of had to take it seriously after a while."[17]

Only the album version of the song has been released, and it has only been played live at eleven concerts.

"PEACE ON EARTH"
Lyrics: Bono
Music: U2
Producer: Lanois/Eno
Additional: Hedges

The Edge calls "Peace on Earth," "one of Bono's most gut-wrenching lyrics."[18] It was written in response to a bombing that took place in August 1998. A car bomb was set off in Omagh, a town in Northern Ireland, by a group opposing the IRA ceasefire and the Good Friday Agreement that looked to bring peace to the country. Twenty-nine people were killed and 220 others were injured.

The Edge has also said it is "the most bitter song U2 has ever written." He shares it "was written in the heat of the moment right after Omagh, I had some music and Bono wrote the lyric in one piece and they just combined to make something very direct and very strong."[19] The vocal was one of the final vocals recorded on the album. The song includes five names, all names of people who were victims in the bombing.

The song also recalls Donna Barker, mother to one of the victims, who spoke about her son's eyes. This led Bono to some of the most heart wrenching lyrics in the song.

The song drew strong emotions when paired with "Walk On" for U2's first performance after the September 11 attacks in the United States as part of the *America: A Tribute to Heroes* telethon, taking place just ten days after the attacks.

"WHEN I LOOK AT THE WORLD"
Lyrics: Bono/Edge
Music: U2
Producer: Eno/Lanois

In *U2 by U2*, Bono speaks about "When I Look at the World," claiming it is about someone faced with tragedy and losing their faith. He remembers when he was sitting in a hospital waiting room when he was young and clouds of smoke when people could still smoke in such environments.[20]

Edge said the song, "started off life as a really heavy full on rock'n'roll arrangement. It sounded too easy in the end. It sounded too predictable for us. We stripped it down. We kind of rearranged it in a much more constrained way."[21]

The song has never been played live by itself in concert, although once in Kansas City, Bono did sing most of the song at the end of "Bad." The "Picante Remix" appeared on a box set celebrating the twentieth anniversary of the album.

"NEW YORK"

Lyrics: Bono
Music: U2
Producer: Eno/Lanois

"New York" is a song about a mid-life crisis, along with an ode to New York City. The song came together quickly, "We only played the song twice ever. The first time was a coming together of the ideas. The second time is the version on the record."[22] The song originated with Eno and Lanois working while U2 were off meeting about other things. U2 liked what they heard when they returned and quickly put the song together. "We all got the studio around 8 a.m. and, one by one, just started playing along with this loop and keyboard part. The song grew out of that."[23]

The "Nice Mix" and "Nasty Mix" appeared on the "Electrical Storm" single, both remixed by Jimmy Cauty of the KLF. The "Carnegie's Deli Remix" and the "Superman Kicks Ativan Remix" by Black Dog were released in the twentieth anniversary box. Both featured additional lyrics not heard on the original album.

"GRACE"

Lyrics: Bono
Music: U2
Producer: Lanois/Eno

"Grace" ends the album. "It's very fresh. It deserves it place on the record very much. But it really had to earn its place on the record because it's very ambient and slow," said The Edge in promotion for the album.[24] The song is the only song on the album which has never been performed live. It did appear over the PA some nights after the shows had ended.

Bono's written the song to discuss the concept of Grace. "It's a word I'm depending on," Bono shares in *U2 by U2*. "The universe operates by Karma, we all know that. For every action there's an equal and opposite reaction. There is some atonement built in: an eye for an eye, a tooth for a tooth. Then enters Grace and turns that upside down. I love it."[25]

Extras from the Era

"Always" and "Summer Rain" featured as B-sides on "Beautiful Day." "Always" was an earlier demo version of "Beautiful Day." "Big Girls Are Best" is a leftover from the *Pop* sessions, produced by Howie B and Flood. The song is an ode to pregnant women, and it appeared as a B-side to "Stuck in a Moment." The remainder of B-sides for the album were live tracks, covers, or remixes.

Bono wrote the screen play of *Million Dollar Hotel* and the soundtrack featured three U2 songs. "The Ground Beneath Her Feet" took lyrics written for a fictional character by Salman Rushdie in his book of the same name. The song is included as a bonus track on some versions of the album. A video was filmed with scenes of Rushdie writing the lyrics, U2 performing in a low-lit hotel room, and scenes from the film. The other new U2 song was "Stateless" a song about being lost and not belonging. "The First Time" from *Zooropa* would also appear.

Three songs from the sessions to record this album appeared in 2004 as part of iTunes' *The Complete U2*. "Levitate," "Love You Like Mad," and "Flower Child." All are poppy songs, and all three could have easily fit on the album. "Levitate" was used to promote the twentieth anniversary release of the album with a lyric video.

In 2002, U2 would release *The Best of 1990–2000* with two new songs. "Electrical Storm" saw U2 working with producer William Orbit. Bono explains, "It's about a couple in a room feeling a storm brewing in the sky outside and equating that to the pressure they feel in their relationship. I think it captures a sense of unease I feel around the world, especially in America, an air of nervous anticipation."[26] The song reached #5 in the UK and #77 in the USA. A video shot in Eze by Anton Corbijn featured a love story between Larry Mullen and a mermaid played by Irish actress Samantha Morton. An alternate mix of "Electrical Storm" titled "The Band Version" was also released. The second new song, also produced by Orbit, was "The Hands That Built America" a song U2 recorded for the film *Gangs of New York*. The lyrics discuss immigrants building America. The song won a Golden Globe for Best Original Song in a Motion Picture, and although nominated for an Academy Award did not win. The song was also nominated, but did not win, for Best Song Written for a Motion Picture, Television or Other Visual Media at the 2004 Grammy Awards. A longer version of the song plays over the final credits of the film.

How to Dismantle an Atomic Bomb (2004)

How to Dismantle an Atomic Bomb was released on November 22, 2004. The album was recorded between February 2003 and July 2004. Work began with producer Chris Thomas and continued through much of 2003. In January 2004, U2 switched gears and invited Steve Lillywhite and Jacknife Lee to join them as producers to rework material they had recorded and to work on some new material for the album. Other producers are credited on the album including Brian Eno, Daniel Lanois, Flood, Carl Glanville, and Nellee Hooper. The album was recorded at U2's studio in Dublin (Hanover Quay) and at their homes in the South of France.

Why the sudden change in direction? In October 2003, the band found themselves working with a twenty-piece orchestra with Thomas heading things up. Larry explained, "It just wasn't there. The songs had a lot of things going for them but they had no magic."[1] Plans for releasing the album were pushed back a year.

The cover is a black-and-white photo of U2 taken at the Concha Bar in Sintra, Portugal by Anton Corbijn. The album design uses black and red throughout and was designed by Shaughn McGrath, with direction by Steve Averill.

The album was released to generally favourable reviews. It debuted at #1 in thirty-four different countries, including the US and the UK. It was awarded Album of the Year and Rock Album of the Year at the 2006 Grammy Awards. It was also awarded Album of the Year at the Meteor Awards, and Best Irish Album at the Hot Press Awards.

The album has not been remastered. Even the most recent release on coloured red vinyl uses the 2004 mastering.

"Vertigo"
Lyrics: Bono/Edge
Music: U2
Producer: Lillywhite

"Vertigo" started life under several different titles including "Hard Metal Jacket," "Full Metal Jacket," "Shark Soup," "Sopa de Tiburon," "Viva La Ramone," and "Native Son."[2] Larry Mullen had developed the drum track in 2002, and The Edge worked on the song with Terry Lawless (a musician who joins U2 on tour) using the track. The track was shared with Bono, who shares how the title became "Shark Soup" on a visit to Chile, "I had a meal in the inn next door where I poisoned myself. I thought I was going to die. It was just me and Guggi, there was no one else in the inn, even the innkeeper had gone home. I was laying on the ground, throwing up at ten-minute intervals and Guggi was trying to get water but it was locked behind the bar."[3] Development continued including lyrics that spoke of Joey Ramone, then Leonard Peltier (see "Native Son" below). When Lillywhite came in as producer he asked Bono if he would be willing to sing the lyrics live in concert, leading Bono to go off and come up with "Vertigo."[4] There are said to be over seventy-five recorded versions of the song.

Bono's definition of "Vertigo":

> It's a dizzy feeling, a sick feeling, when you get up to the top of something and there's only one way to go. That's not a dictionary definition; that's mine. And in my head, I created a club called Vertigo with all these people in it and the music is not the music you want to hear, and the people are not the people you want to be with. And then you just see somebody, and she's got a cross around her neck, and you focus on it—because you can't focus on anything else.[5]

Several remixes of the song were released including mixes by Jacknife Lee, Redanka, and Trent Reznor (Nine Inch Nails).

"Vertigo" was used in a commercial for the Apple iTunes service leading up to the album release. Mark Romanek filmed the ad, featuring the band in silhouette against several colourful backgrounds performing the song. Two weeks after the ads started to be seen, U2 announced a U2-branded iPod, and a digital box set, *The Complete U2*, which would be released through iTunes.

The first video for the song was a simple performance video filmed at U2's studios at Hanover Quay in Dublin. A second video for the song features moving targets in the sand, and evil black sand trails from the band. The video was shot on September 14 and 15 at Punta Del Fangar on the Spanish Mediterranean coast. Alex and Martin direct the video, and with their team build a mini studio in the middle of the sand bar for close-ups and lighting effects. At first the plan was to construct the "target" out of concrete, but due to environmental factors they chose to build with different colours of gravel instead. A third video accompanied the 10-inch remix of the song, featured footage shot during a photo shoot in Portugal. A final video was included with deluxe versions of the album and was called the "Temple Bar Mix"—it features Bono and The Edge playing around with the song, with The Edge on banjo.

In the charts, "Vertigo" did well in the US, reaching #31 in the Billboard Hot 100 and taking #1 in the Alternative Songs chart. In the UK, the song also debuted at #1. "Vertigo" won the Grammy Awards for Best Rock Performance by a Duo or Group with Vocal, Best Rock Song, and Best Short Form Music Video in 2005. "Vertigo" was U2's eighth most streamed song at the end of 2021 on Spotify.

"MIRACLE DRUG"
Lyrics: Bono
Producer: Lillywhite
Additional: Glanville, Lee

"Miracle Drug" is a celebration of science and technology. Christopher Nolan had entered Mount Temple a few years after U2 had gone to school in those halls. Nolan had been born with cerebral palsy and was paraplegic due to issues before birth. A drug allowed him to use a muscle in his neck to communicate by typing. Nolan went on to write several award-winning books.

Bono spoke about the Nolan inspiration, "they attached this unicorn device to his forehead, and he learned to type. And out of him came all these poems that he'd been storing up in his head. Then he put out a collection called *Dam-Burst of Dreams*, which won a load of awards and he went off to university and became a genius. All because of a mother's love and a medical breakthrough."[6] But Bono also admitted the song was not just about Nolan telling *Q Magazine*, "But in a more oblique way it's probably as much about AIDS and the drugs developed to arrest it."[7]

The song appeared in concert regularly during the 2005 tour but was dropped in later legs. U2 would try the song out again at the opening of their 2015 tour but retired it again after only two performances.

"SOMETIMES YOU CAN'T MAKE IT ON YOUR OWN"
Lyrics: Bono
Producer: Thomas
Additional: Lillywhite, Hooper

"Sometimes You Can't Make It on Your Own" was written as a tribute to Bono's father, Bob Hewson, who had died in 2001. An early version of the song, called "Tough," was performed at his father's funeral. Bono spoke about the song, "It's a portrait of him, he was a great singer, a tenor, a working-class Dublin guy who listened to the opera and conducted the stereo with my mother's knitting needles. He just loved opera, so in the song, I hit one of those big tenor notes that he would have loved so much. I think he would have loved it; I hope so."[8]

The song was released as the second single except for North America where the band released "All Because of You." Multiple edits of the song were released to radio, including one at 96 beats per minute, a faster version at 99 beats per minute and another at 103 beats per minute. An earlier demo of the song recorded with Chris Thomas was released via the iTunes set, *The Complete U2*. An acoustic performance of the song was released on the DVD accompanying deluxe versions of the album.

Two videos were filmed with director Phil Joanou. The first version is entirely in black-and-white and features a single take of Bono walking the streets of Dublin singing "Sometimes." The second version used some of the footage from the first version and includes additional footage of the band performing, Bono in the house he grew up in on Cedarwood Road, and on stage at the Gaiety Theatre. Bob Hewson once performed at the Gaiety Theatre himself as a member of the Rathmines and Rathgar Musical Society.

The song reached #97 in the US. In the UK, U2 reached the #1 spot with the song, making this the first album that U2 had reached #1 with two singles. The song won the Best Rock Performance by a Duo or a Group with Vocal and Song of the Year at the 2006 Grammy Awards. The song was also listed at #36 on Q Magazine's Top 100 tracks of 2005.

Taylor Swift has shared that "Sometimes" is her favourite U2 song.

"LOVE AND PEACE OR ELSE"
Lyrics: Bono with The Edge
Producer: Eno, Lanois
Additional: Thomas, Lee, Flood

"Love and Peace or Else" had a difficult birth. The song was started with Daniel Lanois and Brian Eno during sessions for the previous album. The title was first spotted on a list of songs U2 were working on in the summer of 2000 as "Love and Peace (Soul)." The song was developed with Chris Thomas until the band moved on. The song was finished with Jacknife Lee. And at some point, Flood had also been involved.

The song looks at the struggle of war, with Bono looking for love in the light of those conflicts. The song is one of the harder songs on the album. Live in concert Larry would perform this song at the b-stage and when the guitar solo started would head back to his kit on the main stage. Bono would take over for him on drums at the b-stage.

In September 2005, Hurricane Katrina swept into New Orleans leaving the city devastated. As part of the relief efforts U2 participated in a televised concert, performing this song live from their Vertigo stage. It was filmed during a dress rehearsal in Toronto, and later released in audio formats.

"CITY OF BLINDING LIGHTS"
Lyrics: Bono
Producer: Flood
Additional: Thomas, Lee

"City of Blinding Lights" was written about U2's fans. Bono shares, "It's a New York song, about going there for the first time. We were the first band to play Madison Square Gardens after 9/11. During 'Where the Streets Have No Name' the house lights came up and there were 20,000 people in tears. It was beautiful."[9] Bono has also mentioned that there were memories of arriving in London for the first time to play as well. That was something he would explore further in "Invisible."[10]

This song had started development during the sessions for Pop, where it had the name "Scott Walker" and Adam Clayton described it as a homage to the musician.

The song was the third single in most regions but was the fourth in North America. The version issued to radio is an edit of the album version. Two remixes were issued to DJs, the "Paradise Soul Mix" and the "Phones P.D.A. in N.Y.C." mix. The Phones mix was the first time U2 worked with producer Paul Epworth. A remix by Hot Chip would appear on the fan club only album, *Artificial Horizon*.

The song reached #2 on the UK charts, and although it did not reach the Hot 100 chart in the USA, it did reach #40 on the Billboard Adult Pop Songs list.

A video filmed by Alex Courtes and Martin Fougerol was filmed at an arena in Vancouver, BC, over two days. Members of the public were invited to take place and 4,000 fans were allowed into the arena to watch the band perform. The video shows U2 on the Vertigo stage performing the song, incorporating video from the closed set and footage from the Vancouver concert shot the following night.

The song is used on *The Devil Wears Prada* soundtrack. It won Best Rock Song at the 2006 Grammy Awards. The song wont *Hot Press* Awards for the best Irish Single and the best Ringtone. It also reached #42 on *Q Magazine*'s Top 100 tracks of 2005.

"ALL BECAUSE OF YOU"
Lyrics: Bono
Producer: Lillywhite

Bono has not clarified what "All Because of You" is about. Adam Clayton kept things open as well, "It could be about God, it could be about your father or your friends. Or the audience."[11]

The song was the second single in North America, and the fourth single elsewhere. In the UK, it reached #51 as an import on the first release, and #4 when released there. It did not chart on the Hot 100 in the USA but did reach #6 on the Alternative Songs chart.

The second release was of a "Single version" of the song, mixed by Steve Lillywhite, while the album version had been mixed by Flood. An early demo featuring earlier lyrics was released on *The Complete U2*.

The video, directed by Phil Joanou, featured U2 playing the song on the back of a flatbed truck as the truck wound its way through Manhattan. The truck traveled the length of Manhattan, and then crossed into Brooklyn where U2 played a surprise show in the shadow of the Brooklyn Bridge. A second video was filmed during a live performance on the third leg of the Vertigo Tour in Toronto by filmmaker Lian Lunson, but that video has never been released.

"A Man and a Woman"
Lyrics: Bono
Producers: Lee
Additional: Lillywhite, Glanville

Bono explains:

"A Man and A Woman" was about rediscovering a kind of flirtatious and romantic love, when you were younger and less surefooted in the ways that love can take you. It's that dance around the subject, seduction, that beautiful flirtation, which is in the end the most sexual thing, the not knowing, the not going there. Men and women want to trample that mysterious distance that lies between us. I'm intrigued by it; it keeps me interested.[12]

The song was only played once, seven years after it had been released. Bono was performing with The Edge at the "A Decade of Difference" concert honouring former US President Bill Clinton for his sixty-fifth birthday and to celebrate his charitable work. Bono dedicated the song to Clinton's daughter Chelsea and her husband Mark.

An acoustic version of the song featured on the "Walk On" single. This acoustic version is the album version of the song with the bass and drums stripped out of the mix.

"Crumbs from Your Table"
Lyrics: Bono
Producers: Lillywhite
Additional: Lee

"Crumbs from Your Table" was started in Dublin but ended up on a shelf incomplete. One night Bono and The Edge had spent drinking they returned to the song as the sun was rising and started putting the song together.

Bono discussed the lyrics, "I went to speak to Christian fundamentalist groups in America to convince them to give money to fight AIDS in Africa. It was like getting blood from a stone. I told them about a hospice in Uganda where so many people were dying, they had to sleep three to a bed. Sister Anne, who I mention in the song, works at that hospice. Her office is a sewer."[13]

The song has only been played seven times on tour, all on the third leg of the Vertigo Tour. An alternate version performed live in Hanover Quay in Dublin appeared on the bonus DVD that came with deluxe versions of the album.

"One Step Closer"
Lyrics: U2
Producers: Thomas, Lanois
Additional: Lee

"One Step Closer" has a special dedication in the liner notes, "With special thanks to Noel Gallagher." It was Noel who gave Bono the title of the song while speaking about Bono's father who was dying from cancer.

Bono shared, "It was another song for my dad.... The title came from a conversation I was having with Noel Gallagher. We were talking about whether my dad had his faith or not. I said I didn't think he did any more. I thought he had lost it. I wasn't sure he knew where he was going. And Noel said, 'Well he's one step closer to knowing, isn't he?'"[14]

The song has never been performed live in concert, the only song on the album not to be performed.

"Original of the Species"
Lyrics: Bono
Producers: Lillywhite
Additional: Lee

"Original of the Species" celebrated the family of U2's members. It started as a song about The Edge's daughter Hollie, who was the first child of the U2 band members, born during recording *The Unforgettable Fire*. The Edge told *Q Magazine* in 2004, "The last time I cried was listening to that song. It was a song Bono started on the last record about my daughter Hollie. He's her godfather. The lyric became more universal. About being young and full of doubt about yourself. He probably won't agree, but I think it has connotations for Bono, looking back to when he was 20."[15]

"Original of the Species" was the fifth and final song released. No physical singles were released, but it was made available on digital services. The song was rerecorded for the single release, and it is unique to the single. An acoustic version of the song recorded by Bono and The Edge featured on a compilation for the Every Mother Counts Foundation, which seeks to increase childbirth safety for mothers.

A video conceived and directed by Catherine Owens is largely animated with some live footage at the end. It came out of a video piece developed for the Vertigo tour, a rotating digital rendering of a female head with flowers growing out of her mouth. Owens explains that Bono "said to me he wanted to be in a video with her, he wanted to be in her world and have her reflect his world ... and could I make that happen?"[16]

A second video filmed by Mark Pellington in New York featured footage of the band mixed with footage of a live dancer who is visibly pregnant. Some of the footage was also previously seen in the video by Catherine Owens.

The song did not chart in the main US or UK charts, but in the US, it did reach #4 on the Adult Alternative Songs chart. A live version of the song filmed in Chicago was used in a commercial promoting the Apple iPod. An image from the live performance of Bono at the microphone was used for the "Artist" icon in iTunes on Apple mobile devices from 2006–2016.

"Yahweh"

Lyrics: Bono with The Edge
Producer: Thomas

"Yahweh" finishes out the album on a joyous note. Yahweh is a name for the god of the Israelites. Bono explained the use of the word, "I had the idea that no one can own Jerusalem, but everybody wants to put flags on it. The title's an ancient name that's not meant to be spoken. I got around it by singing it. I hope I don't offend anyone."[17]

The song is one of the songs developed with Chris Thomas. An early demo done with Thomas was released on the digital set, *The Complete U2*.

The song was played throughout the Vertigo Tour, although only sporadically on the final leg of the tour. In 2016, The Edge performed at the Sistine Chapel with an Irish choir. "Yahweh" was one of the four songs that he performed. The performance made The Edge the first rock artist to stage a contemporary music concert inside the Chapel. He was attending a regenerative medicine conference being held at the Vatican.

Extras from the Era

The B-side of "Vertigo" was "Are You Gonna Wait Forever?" a song that asks when you are going to get out of your own way and get things done. "Fast Cars" appeared on the album in some countries as a bonus track and contains the lyric which inspired the album title. The song is a strobe light of images taken from the evening news. A remix of "Fast Cars" by Jacknife Lee was also released.

An earlier demo version of "Fast Cars" called "Xanax and Wine" was released with *The Complete U2* on iTunes. It also contained the reference to the album title but is a much rougher version of the song with a different chorus. "Native Son," an early demo of "Vertigo" is also on the collection. Here the lyrics are about Leonard Peltier, an American Indian activist. "Smile" rounds out the new compositions on the digital box set, which Edge claimed arrived too late to be finished. *The Complete U2* also included several early demos of songs released on the album.

"She's a Mystery to Me" was also released as a B-side. The song, written by Bono and The Edge for Roy Orbison, had never been released by U2 themselves. A performance from a surprise promotional show in the shadow of the Brooklyn Bridge gives us our first official release of U2 performing a song written in 1989.

Between albums, U2 issued the compilation *U218 Singles*, which included a cover of "The Saints Are Coming" recorded with Green Day (originally by the Skids) which reached #2 in the UK and #51 in the US. A video for the song, filmed by Chris Milk, sees the band performing at Abbey Road and at the Louisiana Superdome, mixed with Hurricane Katrina footage which has been altered to show what might have happened had the military been deployed to assist in clean up. The song was nominated for, but did not win, Best Rock Performance by a Duo or Group with Vocal at the 2007 Grammy Awards.

The second single from the *U218* compilation was an original song, "Window in the Skies." Both songs came from aborted recording sessions with Rick Rubin. "Window in the Skies" reached #4 in the UK. A video by director Gary Koepke featured footage of musical greats through the years, edited so the lip movements match up to the song lyrics, interspersed with the band being filmed at a concert. Approval to use images of The Beatles came late, and when acquired a second version was done with The Beatles included. Another video directed by Jonas Odell was a 3D animation built from old photos and memorabilia of the band. The song was nominated, but did not win, Best Pop Performance by a Duo or Group with Vocal at the 2008 Grammy Awards (a cover of "Instant Karma" by U2 was also nominated for the same award in the Rock category that year but also did not win).

Two additional songs came out between albums. "Human Rights" is a studio recording that features Bono repeating "everyone" over some backing music, followed by a female voice, Beng Kamsaard from Thailand, reading part of the "The Declaration of Human Rights," released on the *Visionaire 53* Magazine in 2007. And in 2008, U2 joined forces with several Irish artists to sing "The Ballad of Ronnie Drew." Drew was a folk singer and musician who rose to fame with The Dubliners. The tribute to Drew was organized while he was alive and featured Glen Hansard, Sinéad O'Connor, Gavin Friday, The Dubliners, Joe Elliott of Def Leppard, Chris de Burgh, and more. Bono and The Edge were involved in writing the song and all U2 participate in the single, which reached #1 in Ireland.

Above: The European cover of U2's first album *Boy* featured young Peter Rowen on the cover, with the band's name hidden in his hair. The fortieth anniversary edition leaves the U2 off completely. Rowen was photographed by Hugo McGuiness. The album included the single "I Will Follow" and the prior released "Out of Control" and "A Day Without Me." (*Author's collection*)

Below: The North American cover for *Boy* features U2 treated with mirrors and photocopies to stretch the images. The new cover was done when the label expressed concerns about using the photo of Peter Rowen. The photographs of the band were provided by Ian Finlay, and the design was based on U2 tour posters already in use. (*Author's collection*)

Above: The cover of U2's second album *October* featured U2 photographed at the Grand Canal Docks area in Dublin, photographed by Ian Finlay. Windmill Lane Studios was located nearby, and this location is next to where U2 would set up their own studio at Hanover Quay in the 1990s. The album included the singles "Gloria" and "Fire." (*Author's collection*)

Below: The cover of U2's third album *War* saw the return of Peter Rowen, now sporting a split lip, photographed by Ian Finlay. The album included singles "New Year's Day," "Two Hearts Beat as One," "Sunday Bloody Sunday," and, in Germany, "40." (*Author's collection*)

Above: The cover of U2's fourth album *The Unforgettable Fire* features Moydrum Castle near Athlone in Ireland. The castle was burned in 1921 by the IRA leaving it in ruins. It was photographed by Anton Corbijn. The album included singles "Pride (In the Name of Love)," "The Unforgettable Fire," and, in South Africa, "Bad." (*Author's collection*)

Below: The cover of U2's fifth album *The Joshua Tree* features the band at Zabriskie Point, located in Death Valley National Park. The band was photographed by Anton Corbijn. The album included singles "With or Without You," "I Still Haven't Found What I'm Looking For," "Where the Streets Have No Name," and, in North America, "In God's Country." In Australia and New Zealand, "One Tree Hill" was also released. (*Author's collection*)

The cover of U2's seventh album *Achtung Baby* features a grid of photographs by Anton Corbijn taken in Berlin, in studio in Dublin, Santa Cruz de Tenerife, and Tangier. The album included singles "The Fly," "Mysterious Ways," "One," "Even Better Than the Real Thing," and "Who's Gonna Ride Your Wild Horses." Bono stated in 2006 that this is his favourite of the U2 album covers. (*Author's collection*)

Opposite above: The 2017 edition of The Joshua Tree featured an alternate cover featuring a previously unseen photograph of U2 at Zabriskie Point, photographed by Anton Corbijn. The anniversary release also came in a boxed set which featured a silhouette of the Joshua Tree from the back of the original album cover for outer box artwork. (*Author's collection*)

Opposite below: The cover of U2's sixth album *Rattle and Hum*, features a recreation of a scene from the film of the same name, recreated by photographer Anton Corbijn in the studio. The album included singles "Desire," "Angel of Harlem," "When Love Comes to Town," and "All I Want is You." (*Author's collection*)

Above left: The cover for eighth album *Zooropa* is digital art built over a grid of photographs taken from a variety of media sources. The photos include a symbol for nuclear waste, a body builder, lips, and some European dictators. Over the photos is purple text with an early proposed track listing still including mentions of "If God Will Send His Angels," "Wake Up Dead Man," "If You Wear that Velvet Dress," and "Hold Me, Thrill Me, Kiss Me, Kill Me" even though they did not make the album. The ring of digital stars is meant to recall the European flag. And the cartoon character on the front, nicknamed Cosmo, is drawn here by designer Shaughn McGrath, based on artwork by Charlie Whisker. The cover was designed by Steve Averill. The album included singles "Numb," "Lemon," and "Stay (Faraway, So Close!)." (*Author's collection*)

Above right: Original Soundtracks 1 is an album by U2 and Brian Eno, released under the Passengers name. Additional passengers included Pavarotti, Howie B, and Holi. The album cover was designed by Cally at Island Records. The art on the cover is a sci-fi illustration from the 1960s by artist Teodor Rotrekl, originally published in the book *Šest dnů na Luně 1* by Ivo Stuka, published in 1963. The album included the single "Miss Sarajevo." (*Author's collection*)

U2's ninth album *Pop* features photos of the band on the front cover photographed by Anton Corbijn, and treated to appear as "pop art." The album included the singles "Discotheque," "Staring at the Sun," "Last Night on Earth," "Please," "If God Will Send His Angels," and "Mofo." (*Author's collection*)

Above: U2's tenth album *All That You Can't Leave Behind* features a photograph of the band by Anton Corbijn on the front cover. The photograph was taken at Charles de Gaulle airport, Paris. The album included the singles "Beautiful Day," "Stuck in a Moment You Can't Get Out Of," "Elevation," and "Walk On." (*Author's collection*)

Below: U2's eleventh album *How to Dismantle an Atomic Bomb* features a photograph of U2 by Anton Corbijn. The photograph was taken outside the Concha Bar in Sintra, Portugal. The album included the singles "Vertigo," "Sometimes You Can't Make It on Your Own," "All Because of You," "City of Blinding Lights," and "Original of the Species." (*Author's collection*)

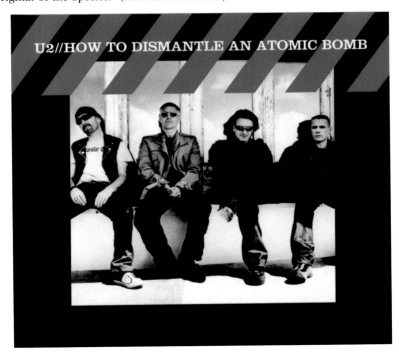

U2's twelfth album *No Line on the Horizon* features a photograph by Japanese artist Hiroshi Sugimoto, part of the artist's Seascapes series. The photograph is an image of the Boden Sea at Uttwil, Switzerland. The band agreed to use the photo as is with no artwork over the photo, and in return the artist was granted to use U2's song "No Line on the Horizon" in future projects. An equals sign, and album titles are placed on the outside of packaging and not on the art itself. The album included the sings "Get on Your Boots," "Magnificent," and "I'll Go Crazy if I Don't Go Crazy Tonight." (*Author's collection*)

U2's thirteenth album *Songs of Innocence* features a photograph of Larry Mullen and his son, Aaron, photographed by Glen Luchford. Early releases for Grammy Awards, and for the free release on iTunes featured a cover that looks like a white label record, but also features the shoulder tattoo that can be seen on Larry's shoulder in the final cover. The tattoo design is from Native American mythology and is a symbol of protecting the innocents. The album included the singles "The Miracle (Of Joey Ramone)," "Every Breaking Wave," and "Song for Someone." (*Author's collection*)

U2's fourteenth album *Songs of Experience* features a photograph by Anton Corbijn of two young people holding hands, while the girl wears an army helmet reminiscent of one Peter Rowen wore in earlier album artwork. The girl is Sian Evans, daughter of The Edge. The boy is Eli Hewson, Bono's son. The album included the singles "You're the Best Thing About Me," "The Blackout," "Get Out of Your Own Way," "Lights of Home," "Love is Bigger Than Anything in its Way," and "Summer of Love." (*Author's collection*)

U2 performing during the closing show of the Vertigo tour in Honolulu, Hawaii, December 2006. (*Aaron J. Sams*)

The Edge (aka David Evans) performing in Dublin during the U2360° tour, July 2009. The Edge plays guitar, keyboards, and handles backing vocals in U2. "The Edge" was a nickname given to Evans as a teen, said to be derived from his sharp facial features. (*Aaron J. Sams*)

Bono (aka Paul Hewson) performing in Dublin during the Joshua Tree 2017 tour, July 2017. Bono is the lead vocalist and plays guitar in U2. The nickname "Bono Vox" is Latin for "Good Voice" and is taken from the name of a Dublin hearing aid shop. (*Aaron J. Sams*)

Adam Clayton performing in Amsterdam during the Joshua Tree 2017 tour, July 2017. Adam Clayton is the bassist in U2. Being the oldest in the band, Adam was the first to turn his attention to music full time, taking on the role of the first manager of the band. (*Aaron J. Sams*)

Larry Mullen performing in Boston during the Innocence + Experience tour, July 2015. Larry Mullen is the drummer in U2 and contributes the odd backing vocal. It was Larry Mullen who started the band, posting a note to the high school bulletin board, inviting other students interested in starting a band to join him at his home on Rosemount Avenue on September 25, 1976. (*Aaron J. Sams*)

Above: The red screens have been used for many concert tours to introduce "Where the Streets Have No Name." Here the song is performed during the Joshua Tree 2017 tour in Amsterdam, the Netherlands, July 2017. (*Aaron J. Sams*)

Left: The Edge during "Vertigo" which uses a red and black bullseye pattern on screens as the song is performed. Amsterdam, the Netherlands, July 2017. (*Aaron J. Sams*)

Bono performing "Hold Me, Thrill Me, Kiss Me, Kill Me" during the U2360° tour in Toronto, July 2011. (*Aaron J. Sams*)

Adam Clayton performing "Ultra Violet (Light My Way)" in Seattle, during a Joshua Tree 2017 show, May 2017. (*Aaron J. Sams*)

Larry Mullen performing the rarely heard "The Troubles" in Vancouver, during a Joshua Tree 2017 show, May 2017. (*Aaron J. Sams*)

U2 perform at the Garden, in Boston, MA, as part of the Experience + Innocence tour in June 2018. (*Aaron J. Sams*)

Above: U2 perform at Croke Park, in Dublin, as part of the U2360° tour in July 2009. (*Aaron J. Sams*)

Right: Bono as "The Shadowman." the character he assumed for the performance of "Exit" during shows on the Joshua Tree tour, photographed in Dublin in July 2017. (*Aaron J. Sams*)

U2 perform a special show at the Apollo Theatre in July 2018. The show is recorded and released in full as a fan club release via U2.com. Here the band is accompanied by the Sun Ra Arkestra, celebrating the thirtieth anniversary of *Rattle and Hum*. (*Aaron J. Sams*)

U2 take a moment to say goodbye to their audience at the end of the American tour leg of the Experience + Innocence tour, held in Uncasville, CT. (*Aaron J. Sams*)

No Line on the Horizon
(2009)

No Line on the Horizon was released on February 27, 2009. Initial recording for the album with Rick Rubin in 2006 was shelved, and the band continued with long time collaborators Brian Eno and Daniel Lanois, not only as producers but also as musicians and co-writers. The album was first developed on a trip to Fez in Morocco, and later developed in New York, London, and Dublin. Additional production work involved Steve Lillywhite, Declan Gaffney, and will.i.am. Deluxe versions of the album came with a film developed by Anton Corbijn using the songs from the album, titled *Linear*.

Initial plans called for the album to be a double album, with one disc being "daylight" and the other "darkness," or later "sunrise" and "sunset." The album was postponed from 2008, and at the time it was decided to focus on material for a single album. The additional songs were to be held for a follow up album *Songs of Ascent*.

The cover of the album is a black-and-white photograph by Japanese artist Hiroshi Sugimoto, taken in 1993 and titled "Boden Sea" (Lake Constance in Europe). A deal was reached between the band and Sugimoto in which he could use the music from *No Line on the Horizon* in his future projects. Sugimoto did make one request, relating what he told Bono: "Are you sure? If you use it you won't be able to put anything on top of it, not even the U2 name."[1] These items were either on a slip case or a sticker outside the cover. The album art was designed by Shaughn McGrath and Steve Averill, continuing their long-term relationship with U2.

The album debuted at #1 in thirty countries. Sales of the album were less than anticipated, however, and the band expressed disappointment in those sales compared to previous albums. However, upon the release of Coldplay's *Mylo Xyloto* in 2011, *Billboard* magazine was using *No Line on the Horizon* as the measure of success for rock album sales, noting that Coldplay's album had not sold as well as U2's. The album was awarded the Grammy for Best Rock Album in 2010. *Rolling Stone* also placed the album at the #1 spot in its list of the Best Albums of 2009.

A remastered version of the album was released in 2019 on vinyl to celebrate the tenth anniversary of the album.

"No Line on the Horizon"
Lyrics: Bono
Music: U2, Eno, Lanois
Producer: Eno/Lanois
Additional: Lillywhite

The opening track gives the album its name. Bono described it as "that moment, if you live by the sea, which I do in Dublin, Killiney Bay, and the sea and sky become the same colour. It happens every so often, you just lose the line on the horizon and you disappear into infinity. It's a sort of meditative thing really, it just became quite a hopeful image, about no end in sight, whether that's a relationship, or whether that's a band. There's no end in sight."[2] The song was born during U2's trip to Fez and was described as an ambient Eno-esque song from those sessions.

A second version with a faster tempo version was released called, "2." This is not a remix but rather a separate recording, including some lyrics changes. The faster version was finished with Eno, Cenzo Townshend, and will.i.am from the Black Eyed Peas, who also contributes some vocals. The faster mix was available on the album as a bonus track.

Bono describes the song as "It's the Buzzcocks meets Bow Wow Wow."[3] Daniel Lanois calls it "Space age rock and roll—space age rockabilly" and The Edge calls it "raw and very to-the-point."[4, 5]

"Magnificent"
Lyrics: Bono and The Edge
Music: U2, Eno, Lanois
Producer: Eno/Lanois
Additional: Lillywhite

"Magnificent" took shape in the sessions in Fez under the name "French Disco." The Edge talked about the start of the song, "I think we all knew it was inherently joyful, which is rare. We had a group of Moroccan percussionists in at the time. They played along with us, and what was already a very rhythmic jam went onto another level of sophistication."[6] Lanois adds, "That was born in Fez. We wanted to have something euphoric, and Bono came up with that little melody. And he loved that melody and stuck with it. Almost like a fanfare."[7]

"Magnificent" was the second single and featured several remixes of the title track by Richard Vission, Fred Falke, Dave Audé, Adam K and Soha, Pete Tong, and Redanka. In a surprise, "Magnificent" was released as a CD single in the US, the first physical release of a single there since the "Vertigo" 7-inch in 2004, and the first CD-single release in the US since 1997. Two different edits of "Magnificent" were sent to radio for promotion. A remix by will.i.am that Bono called "the most extraordinary" remix has never been released.[8]

A video directed by Alex Courtes was filmed in Fez, Morocco, opens with buildings in the city covered by a large white cloth, shots of people dancing, and U2 performing in a riad. The sheets are pulled from the building as the video progresses and blow over the Fez skyline. A second video, also directed by Courtes adds more footage of the band walking around Fez, and a greater focus on the riad recording sessions. The riad used for filming appears to be different than Riad El Yacout where U2 had worked on the album. A third video, filmed by Tom Krueger, was taken from U2's promotional performance at Somerville Theatre in Boston.

"Magnificent" reached #42 on the UK charts. In the US, it did not chart on the Hot 100 but charted on the Rock Songs chart (#33), Adult Pop Charts (#23), Alternative Charts (#18), and the Dance/Club Play Charts (#2). "Magnificent" is one of two songs from the album which have been played since the end of the U2360° Tour.

"MOMENT OF SURRENDER"

Lyrics: Bono
Music: U2, Eno, Lanois
Producer: Eno/Lanois

"Moment of Surrender" was born while the band was jamming and recorded on the spot. Eno said the song was "hatched almost fully formed in a breathtaking few hours, the most amazing studio experience I've ever had."[9] The song was edited down from a longer recording, and a short cello piece in the intro was added later, but "the song appears on the album exactly as it was the first and only time we played it."[10]

Daniel Lanois, Steve Lillywhite and Adam Clayton all name the song as their favourite from the album.[11] "Moment of Surrender" was considered for a fourth single from the album, but the band decided to stop after three. Work had been done editing the song down for radio, and some remixes had been commissioned.

If you listen carefully you may hear some rougher moments in the track, Larry shares, "That was one take, it was done in 15 minutes. As I'm going through it the electronic drum kit breaks, so it's broken, and I'm trying to fix it. So, when you hear the drums isolated, you hear me struggling to get this thing fixed. Which is always good, just makes it a little more interesting."[12]

The song ended the concerts on the U2360° Tour. During the song, Bono would often insert an extended rap. The extended rap was also included during the song's performance on *Saturday Night Live*. "Moment of Surrender" was the other song from the album which was performed live after the end of the U2360° Tour, as Bono performed the song with Mary J. Blige at a fundraising event in 2013.

"Unknown Caller"
Lyrics/Music: U2/Eno/Lanois
Producer: Eno/Lanois
Additional: Lillywhite

"Unknown Caller" was one of the songs which came to fruition in Fez. Lanois spoke about the genesis of the track, "There was no monkey business, it pretty much had its personality intact from day one. And a pretty great vocal from early."[13] The Edge described, "The idea is that the narrator is in an altered state, and his phone starts talking to him."[14] Answering a question about his favourite song on the album, The Edge named "Unknown Caller."[15]

Some elements of the recording environment are present, you can hear birds as the song opens. Bono shared with *Q Magazine*, "We took over this little hotel, that they call a riad, and set up the gear in the courtyard. So, it was open, a square of sky over our heads. You can hear the call to prayer, birds flying around. Two swallows came back regularly to shit on Larry's drums."[16]

Like "Moment of Surrender" the song was also considered a possible single release. A remix of the song was completed by Snow Patrol and was available as a digital download when purchasing the remix album *Artificial Horizon*.

"I'll Go Crazy If I Don't Go Crazy Tonight"
Lyrics: Bono
Music: U2
Producer: Lillywhite
Additional: will.i.am

Bono expressed that the album worked in three pieces, "very unusual first third is a whole world onto itself, you get to a very ecstatic place. Then there's a load of singles like *Rubber Soul*, like 'Get on Your Boots'. Then the last third goes into some very unusual territory I think is worth visiting."[17] "I'll Go Crazy If I Don't Go Crazy Tonight" opens the middle third of the album. The song initially developed with Brian Eno under the name "Diorama," but the band took it away reworking it with Steve Lillywhite and will.i.am from the Black Eyed Peas who also contributes keyboards.

Will.i.am took some of the ideas for the song back to his work with the Black Eyed Peas. Interscope label boss Jimmy Iovine revealed, "I sent will.i.am over to the studio to do some remixes on 'I'll Go Crazy'. He works on them for two weeks, comes back and writes 'I Gotta Feeling'. The chords are U2 chords, 100 per cent. Will even told them."[18] The Peas song was a massive hit in North America. The band would open for U2 during the U2360° Tour.

Bono reveals "there's a lot of mischief on this record" when speaking about the song. He has identified that he was inspired by U2 fans involved in campaigning for Obama, but also wanted to have fun with the song. "It's the final blow to people who can't stand us. That we seem to be having a better time than everyone else as well. It's like, it's not enough not to have broken up, to have made some hopefully inspiring music over the years, but also to be having a lot of fun. The mischief is part of our story and it isn't represented or read about."[19] The band did have fun with this song. They worked with Redanka and Dirty South to remix the song for live performances complete with dancing heads on the screen. To many fans it was a highlight of the tour, and one group of fans had their own synchronized dance to accompany the lyrics each night.

The song was the third and final single from the album. A number remixes by Redanka, Dirty South, and Fish Out of Water were completed for the single. The song reached #32 in the UK Charts. It did not chart in the US.

The first video was a live version taken from the performance at the second night of the tour in Barcelona. The band played the song twice that evening, first playing the remixed version, and later during the encore playing a version of the song closer to what had appeared on the album. Close ups were filmed during soundcheck, and live action during the actual concert. A second animated video followed, directed by David O'Reilly, an Irish filmmaker. The video follows several animated characters, all on a path to change their lives, who cross paths during the video.

"I'll Go Crazy If I Don't Go Crazy Tonight" was featured in an ad for BlackBerry, a manufacturer of phones. The ad featured footage of the band performing the song live with impressive light effects. BlackBerry was also one of the tour sponsors and developed an app to accompany the tour. The ad campaign was titled "BlackBerry Loves U2."

The song was nominated but did not win Best Rock Song and Best Rock Performance by a Duo or Group with Vocal at the 2010 Grammy Awards.

"GET ON YOUR BOOTS"
Lyrics: Bono
Music: U2
Producers: Eno/Lanois
Additional: Gaffney

"Get on Your Boots" according to Bono was a "sassy, lightweight, kind of a Polaroid of a family at a carnival.... It's kind of sentimental but around it you sense this foreboding..."[20] The song recalls a night that Bono himself was on a family holiday in the South of France, and they could hear the start of the Iraq War, with planes moving overhead.

Edge developed the guitar riff in his home, and then later involved Larry Mullen working in studio. The early progress of the song can be seen in the documentary *It Might Get Loud*, which looked at the working style of The Edge, Jack White, and Jimmy Page. Lanois remembers the chant in the song, "It was something Bono was toying with—that we are children of the sound. Having been at it for as long as he has, he realizes how special the gift is to be moved by music and that we live in the sound. That's what we resonate with and what we are as artisans and artist. A gratefulness and a realization."[21]

"Get on Your Boots" was released as a single six weeks before the album. The world premiere was set to happen on RTÉ 2fm but when a snippet of the track was leaked on the internet the song was quickly made available online prior to the first play. This marked the first time U2 made a single available on iTunes the same day as delivery to radio, usually the iTunes releases had been timed to be released the same day as the commercial single. "Get on Your Boots" was the last CD single issued by U2 in Canada and Australia/New Zealand.

A video directed by Alex Courtes featured the band performing in studio among images of the universe, with images suggested by the lyric appearing behind them. An unfinished version of the video had been leaked to YouTube early. This rough version still had Getty Images watermarks in some places where artwork had not been cleared, as well as a few unobstructed shots of topless models. In the final version of the video, the models' breasts are obscured, a few other sexually suggestive shots have been toned down, and the watermarks are gone. A second unreleased video, directed by Martyn Pick, features the same band performance footage from the Courtes video, uses a different background treatment with muted reds and yellows and images suggestive of pop art. A third video, by Catherine Owens was used to promote the song using a longer mix of the song. The lyric footage was also used by the band for promotional performances of the song, including the Grammy Awards and the Brit Awards.

The single reached #12 in the UK charts and reached #37 on the *Billboard* Hot 100 in the United States, as well as charting on the Alternative Songs (#5) and Pop Songs (#27) charts.

"STAND UP COMEDY"
Lyrics: Bono
Music: U2
Producer: Eno/Lanois
Additional: Lillywhite

"Stand Up Comedy" was inspired by the Stand Up and Take Action Campaign, a campaign against poverty. Bono explains, "it's inspired by this concept of stand up. It's a little diamond, though. It's not a 'let's hold hands and the world is a better place sort of song.' It's more kick down the door of your own hypocrisy."[22]

The song was developed in Fez under the title "For Your Love" and finished late in the recording sessions. Lanois explained, "That song went through a lot of changes—that song was about six different songs. It's a study in itself—it would be a cool full-length CD—just the evolution of 'Stand Up Comedy'. It was another song all together. A great song. But in the end, it felt crafted—more craft than soul. And we like to make soul music."[23] Eno has also commented on the painful birth of the song, "It can be frustrating at times when they sometimes take a song and work it into the ground, then work it back to life again. That's what happened with 'Stand Up Comedy'. I was thinking the other day that Edge has probably heard that song more times than even the most dedicated U2 fan ever will."[24]

The song is one of four on the album never played live in concert.

"FEZ – BEING BORN"
Lyrics: Bono
Music: U2, Eno, Lanois
Producer: Eno/Lanois

"Fez – Being Born" developed under the names "Chromium Chords" and "Tripoli." The chant from "Get on Your Boots" returns in this song. Lanois explains the title, "Bono thought that it had this feeling like it was almost something coming to life. Like a flower opening or coming into the world and then into the Being Born section. That's the high-speed rhythmic part."[25]

The album recording had started in Fez. Bono spoke about the importance of location, "I've learned from poets really. Find a physical location and suddenly the book of poetry will gather around it."[26] The ideas certainly flowed in Fez. Larry Mullen would tell Larry Gogan about the work in Fez, "We worked through 100–150 ideas. Some of them ended up on the album, some of them didn't."[27]

"Fez - Being Born" is the second song of four on the album which has never been performed in concert.

"WHITE AS SNOW"
Lyrics: U2, Eno, Lanois
Music: Traditional
Producers: Eno/Lanois

"White as Snow" takes the music from the Christian hymn, "O Come, O Come, Emmanuel" and adds new lyrics. The original hymn is one that is used for Advent and Christmas arranged here by Eno and Lanois.

Lanois found the hymn, "After my conversation with Bono about future hymns or future spirituals, I did a little studying. In fact, with a friend in Toronto, Lori Anna Reid—she's a great singer from Toronto and she's quite an expert on spirituals. I asked her to fish a few out for me and we had a listening session and that one stood out to me."[28] In the meantime, U2 had been asked to write a song for a new Jim Sheridan film, *Brothers* and they ended up writing two, "White as Snow" and "Winter." Sheridan chose to use "Winter."

It is the third song on the album which has never been performed live in concert.

The song was one of the last finished. The Edge revealed: "In the last 48 hours of the recording we did 7 mixes, and Bono did 2 vocals, and we wrote lyrics to a song 'White as Snow' where we only had sketch lyrics before."[29]

"Breathe"
Lyrics: Bono
Music: U2
Producer: Lillywhite
Additional: Lanois/Eno

Although "Breathe" was mostly developed, the song was only recorded in full in the final two weeks of work. Although not credited, work was done on the song with will.i.am as well. Bono speaking about the song stated, "I enjoyed playing with other characters. As it happens, I am from a long line of traveling sales people on my mother's side. I genuinely see myself as a traveling sales person, whether selling melodies, or selling ideas like debt cancellation" says Bono of the song.[30] It is his favourite of the album, identified as such in several interviews, "It's like a storm blows up!"[31]

A number of different mixes of "Breathe" were completed with quite varied lyrics. One of these alternative recordings with lyrics that focus on Nelson Mandela was issued as a B-side on "Ordinary Love." Another version appeared in the *Miracle Rising: South Africa* documentary when it aired on the History Channel. Alternative lyrics for "Breathe" can be found in the booklet that accompanies the deluxe versions of the album.

"Breathe" would open early dates on the U2360° Tour. Larry Mullen would take the stage and open the concert with a barrage of drums to open the shows before the rest of the band would join him.

When asked by Jo Whiley of their favourite songs on the album, both Larry and Bono name "Breathe."[32]

"Cedars of Lebanon"
Lyrics: Bono
Music: U2, Eno, Lanois
Producer: Lanois

"Cedars of Lebanon" closes the album and samples heavily from another song. "Against the Sky" was a song that Harold Budd recorded with Brian Eno and Daniel Lanois in 1984. The U2 song is layered over top of the ambient piece that is "Against the Sky." "I always loved this particular track on *The Pearl*, so I based the mood of Cedars on kind of an excerpt from *The Pearl*. And then Larry Mullen came in with a killer drum part on that, I was really proud of him. I love the mood on that track; it's really thick with ambience. Almost like a direct throwback to the early 80s, to what I was doing with Eno. I'm proud of it, it's a nice revisit to that work," explains Lanois.[33]

Bono's lyrics are written as a character, a war correspondent writing from the war. "The journalist in this picture is not really writing about what's going on in Lebanon, he's writing about his own apocalypse, in his personal life…. It's a very bleak end to not a bleak album" says Bono of the song.[34]

The song is one of four never performed in concert.

Extras from the Era

"Winter" was cut from the album so late in the project that it was already used in Anton Corbijn's film *Linear* accompanying the album in deluxe formats. The song was written for Jim Sheridan's film *Brothers*, and two versions were developed, a rock arrangement heard in *Linear*, and an acoustic arrangement used in *Brothers*. The song was nominated for a Golden Globe Award in 2010.

"Soon" is one of the songs held back for *Songs of Ascent*. Initially developed as a song called "Kingdom of my Love" the song could be heard as U2 took the stage during the U2360° Tour. A special 7-inch red vinyl of the song was included with the boxed set of the Rose Bowl home video.

"Mercy" had been cut late from *How to Dismantle an Atomic Bomb*, and leaked in 2004, becoming a fan favourite. In 2010, as the band continued their U2360° Tour in Europe, they debuted several new songs live in concert. "Mercy" debuted in concert in Zurich, and to Bono's surprise many of the fans sang along. One performance was released on the EP "Wide Awake in Europe" released for the Record Store Black Friday Event in 2010. The other new songs debuting in concert were "The Return of the Stingray Guitar" (later developed to become "Lucifer's Hands"); "Glastonbury" (later developed to become "Volcano" and "American Soul"); "Every Breaking Wave"; "North Star"; and "Boy Falls from the Sky."

"North Star" has never been released; however, it can be heard in the film *Transformers 3: Dark of the Moon*. U2 planned an album in 2011 with "North Star" as a single when the film hit theatres. The album was pushed back, but the song remained in the film. At the time the song was described to celebrate Johnny Cash's faith. It has been announced Bono and The Edge will lend a song to Jim Sheridan's semi-autobiographical film *North Star*. "Boy Falls from the Sky" was released, but not a recording by U2, rather as part of the *Spider-Man: Turn off the Dark* Broadway performance and accompanying soundtrack. The song was developed by U2, and it is U2 credited with the music. The other songs in the musical did not have any input from Adam Clayton or Larry Mullen.

14

Songs of Innocence (2014)

Songs of Innocence was released on September 9, 2014 via iTunes as a free album. The album was announced that day at an Apple Keynote address and was available to fans moments later. Physical copies of the album were released in most countries a month later, after Apple enjoyed a month of exclusive rights to the album. Apple paid U2 an undisclosed sum to carry the album for that period.

When *No Line on the Horizon* was split into two albums the second album of material was identified as *Songs of Ascent*. The band worked on that material for several years but eventually put it into the vault and started fresh working on new material with Danger Mouse for the album that would become *Songs of Innocence* ("Every Breaking Wave" was the only song to make the jump to this new project). The album was recorded at Electric Lady and Pull Studios in New York, with additional recording completed in London, Los Angeles, and Dublin. When Danger Mouse had to depart due to other commitments, the band worked with Paul Epworth and later Ryan Tedder (of OneRepublic fame) to complete the album. Long-time collaborators Flood and Declan Gaffney also receive production credits on the album.

For iTunes, the cover of the album was an image of a vinyl record in a white die cut sleeve. The "sun" symbol on the cover is an image taken from Larry Mullen's shoulder tattoo. The physical copies of the album were released with a photo of a shirtless Larry Mullen holding his son, Aaron. Larry is posed so his tattoo is prominent in the photo. The tattoo is a design from Native American mythology and is a symbol of protecting the innocent. Deluxe versions of the album were released with several acoustic tracks, additional mixes, and two new songs, and "Invisible" as a hidden track. The album design work was by Shaughn McGrath with Steve Averill.

Due to the free giveaway for a month, U2 were not eligible for the charts until the physical version was released. This resulted in the album debuting at #4 in the UK Charts and did not chart in the US.

Much of the press surrounding the album focused on the delivery through iTunes overshadowing the album itself. The original idea was to give people free access to the album, but many people found an album they did not want on their devices if they had automatic downloads turned on. More troubling, people struggled to remove the album, it kept returning. There was a strong outcry and three days after the album was released Apple issued an update allowing users to delete the album.

A special release in black vinyl in very limited quantities was done through two stores in North America to allow the album to be considered for the 2015 Grammy Awards. For Record Store Day, a black vinyl edition of the album was issued in limited quantities (the normal commercial version is in white vinyl).

"THE MIRACLE (OF JOEY RAMONE)"
Lyrics: Bono/Edge
Music: U2
Producer: Danger Mouse/Epworth/Tedder

"The Miracle (of Joey Ramone)" was performed at an Apple keynote event in California to announce the new iPhone. The band announced their album, and that it would be free on iTunes for a month at the event.

Joey Ramone fronted the Ramones. Like other songs on the album, this one takes U2 back to their early days. Bono shares, "I found my voice through Joey Ramone because I wasn't the obvious punk-rock singer, or even rock singer. I sang like a girl—which I'm into now, but when I was 17 or 18, I wasn't sure. And I heard Joey Ramone, who sang like a girl, and that was my way in."[1] The song is based on a real-life concert experience for the band. Bono shared:

> The 4 members of U2 went to see the Ramones playing in the State Cinema in Dublin without thinking about how we were going to get in. We had no tickets and no money.... My best friend Guggi had a ticket and he snuck us through a side exit he pried open. The world stopped long enough for us to get on it. Even though we only saw half the show, it became one of the great nights of our life...[2]

The song was the first single from the album but did not make the UK charts because the song was available free via iTunes and not sold. In the US, it did not chart on the Hot 100 but appeared on the Adult Alternative (#1), Rock Airplay (#12), Hot Rock (#42), and Alternative Songs (#42) charts.

An ad by director Mark Romanek featured the band performing in studio, the footage was colourized and presented on a white background with images of the Ramones performing, and was used to promote iTunes. Additional footage from that day was used by Digital Air, creating a full-length music video for the song. The video sees U2 performing the song in studio, with a variety of visual effects overlaid on the performance.

An acoustic version of the song titled the "Busker Version" appeared on deluxe versions of the album. A remix titled the "Miraculous Medal Mix" was played after several shows on the 2018 Experience + Innocence Tour, a studio version of the remix has not been issued.

"EVERY BREAKING WAVE"
Lyrics: Bono/Edge
Music: U2
Producer: Danger Mouse/Tedder
Additional: Gaffney

"Every Breaking Wave" was developed for *No Line on the Horizon*. Previews of the album had Bono calling the song "early electronica" and commenting "you don't hear indie bands doing blue-eyed soul."[3] Late in the recording of that album, it was decided to split the album into two, and to hold "Every Breaking Wave" as the lead single when the second album was released. Although it took longer than expected, the song did make the next album. In between, the song had a live debut in 2010 on the U2360° Tour. The version appearing here was newly recorded for the album. Credits for the song reveal that Bono plays the dulcimer on the song.

Bono has described the song as being a story about characters who give themselves fully to another person and the problems that can come from that.[4]

The song was the second single on radio. An edit was sent to radio in late 2014, and a new mix of the song was sent to radio in early 2015. This new mix was also available to download via the band's website and was commercially released on digital services in 2019.

An acoustic version of the song appeared on deluxe versions of the album. An earlier alternate mix of the song leaked as part of the promotion for U2's *Films of Innocence* project when the video for the song streamed on Complex, featuring an early, watermarked, version of the song. It was quickly removed and replaced with the proper version later that day.

A music video, filmed by Aoife McArdle came in two versions, a thirteen-minute film and a shorter four-minute video. The video was filmed in Belfast and featured a love story of two young people caught on opposite sides during the Troubles in the 1970s. A third video of the band performing in Metropolis Studios was also released.

No commercial single was released in the UK and the song did not chart. In the US, it did not make the Hot 100 but appeared on the Adult Top 40 (#34), Adult Contemporary (#28), and the Adult Alternative Songs (#7) charts. *Rolling Stone* named the song as #3 in the best songs of 2014 and #49 in their Best Songs of the 2010s list. The song was U2's eleventh most streamed song at the end of 2021 on Spotify.

Actress and singer Juliette Lewis has named "Every Breaking Wave" as one of her favourite U2 songs.

"CALIFORNIA (THERE IS NO END TO LOVE)"
Lyrics: Bono/Edge
Music: U2
Producer: Gaffney/Epworth/Danger Mouse

"California (There is No End to Love)" opens with a Beach Boys-esque chant and Bono says, "it's like the sun itself."[5] The song is a love letter to California, "it's about our first trip to Los Angeles," says Bono, another song looking back at U2's earliest days.[6] Backing vocals include Declan Gaffney and Larry Mullen.

"We wanted to make a very personal album, let's try to figure out why we wanted to be in a band, the relationships around the band, our friendships, our lovers, our family. The whole album is first journeys—first journeys geographically, spiritually, sexually," Bono explained about revisiting the earliest days.[7]

An acoustic version was released on deluxe versions of the album.

"SONG FOR SOMEONE"
Lyrics: Bono/Edge
Music: U2
Producer: Tedder/Flood

"Song for Someone" is about Bono's wife Ali, and the single featured a picture of a young Ali on the cover. Bono told Dave Fanning that the song is about "the awkwardness of falling in love and sex."[8] Ali and Bono started dating around the same time that U2 had formed, and have remained together ever since, marrying in 1982. When writing the album, Bono wanted to answer the question "Why are you like this?" by looking at his earliest experiences.[9]

The song was the third and final single sent to radio and made available on streaming services. A "radio mix" of the song was released, remixed by The Edge, increasing the loudness of the backing vocals. Bono joked that the mix was pretty much unchanged. It was accompanied by a live version recorded in San Jose.

A film directed by Vincent Haycock featured Woody Harrelson as Aaron Brown who is being released from prison. He is met outside by his daughter, played by Harrelson's own daughter Zoe. The film was nine minutes long, and a shorter four-minute edit was also created. A second video, directed by Matt Mahurin, is a black-and-white video featuring on light and darkness. Bono is the only member of the band featured. A third video filmed by Chris Milk at a soundcheck in Toronto uses 360-degree cameras allowing the viewer to move around and look at different things in VR. The song is performed by the band, joined by other musicians around the world.

The song "13 (There is a Light)" on *Songs of Experience* revisits "Song for Someone."

"Iris (Hold Me Close)"
Lyrics: Bono/Edge
Music: U2
Producer: Epworth/Tedder
Additional: Danger Mouse

Iris Hewson, Bono's mother, died when Bono was fourteen. She had passed away at her own father's funeral. *Songs of Innocence* was released forty years to the day after her death by coincidence. Iris has been a focus of several previous songs including "I Will Follow," "Tomorrow," "Mofo," and "Lemon."

Bono spoke with Dave Fanning about the song, "Sometimes the things that have the most powerful influence over you are from way back. You're looking at the night sky and those beautiful stars—a lot of them are gone, even though you're still in their light."[10]

Live in concert old video footage of Bono's mother was shown on the screens as the band performs. The lyrics from "Iris" are revisited on *Songs of Experience* in "Lights of Home."

"Volcano"
Lyrics: Bono/Edge
Music: U2
Producer: Gaffney
Additional: Epworth

U2 were booked to appear at the 2010 Glastonbury Festival. The band had started work on a song for the festival, called "Glastonbury." Although they had to cancel their appearance that year, the song did debut on tour in 2010, and was later taken back into studio and reworked becoming "Volcano."

Bono discussed that "Volcano" came from rage, "you know we were talking about grief, but after grief comes rage. Volcano … Volcano follows 'Iris' on the album. And that's a lot to do with that rage. Where do you put that rage? You put that rage into being in a band. Into rock and roll."[11] Bono discussed turning that rage into music, "Music arrives in my life as an emancipation and punk rock gives me a place to howl. And it's alchemy. It's literally turning your shit into gold records."[12]

Larry Mullen also lost his mom as the band was starting:

> Everything was broken. Like home, that was just gone, everything was gone. So, my thing was to find somewhere else to go. I needed another family, and the band became that for me, and it was a refuge. I was sitting behind a drumkit. I didn't have to explain myself. And that's been very convenient because it's not easy stuff to talk about, and I admire Bono for doing it.[13]

"Raised by Wolves"

Lyrics: Bono/Edge
Music: U2
Producer: Gaffney/Danger Mouse

"Raised by Wolves" tackles the Troubles that were being felt throughout Ireland as U2 were growing up. The incident detailed in the song happened in Dublin in 1974. A loyalist paramilitary group called the Ulster Volunteer Force set off three car bombs that went off during rush hour in Dublin, and a fourth bomb in Monaghan. Thirty-three people were killed, including an unborn child, and 300 were injured. The second bomb that went off was inside a Ford Escort, parked on Talbot Street, license plate 1385 WZ which is referenced in the song.

Bono revealed, "It was very disturbing to realize that my teenage life was largely dominated by memories of violence and that my worldview was shaped by that. It might mean some sort of psychological flaw in me, but I feel most comfortable in the middle of the biggest, noisiest, most chaotic, howling argument."[14]

Where was Bono on that day? "The bombs were set to go off at the same time on a Friday evening, at 5.30pm," Bono shared. "At that time on Fridays in 1974 I would have been at the Golden Discs shop in Marlborough Street, just around the corner from where the bombs exploded. But that day I had cycled to school so didn't get the bus into town afterwards as usual."[15]

The song was played on tour in 2015 and 2018, complete with a car on screen and the sound of explosions shaking the arena. A quieter acoustic version of the song can be found on the deluxe version of the album.

"Cedarwood Road"

Lyrics: Bono/Edge
Music: U2
Producer: Danger Mouse/Epworth

Cedarwood Road was the street that Bono lived on as a child. His family lived at No. 10. Two life-long friends were from the street, Gavin Friday at No. 140 and Guggi at No. 5. The cherry blossom tree that Bono mentions stood outside Guggi's house.

Not all the memories of childhood were positive. The seven towers mentioned in "Running to Stand Still" were built nearby and many families were moved from the inner city to the neighborhood along with reports of several social problems. Bono would remember "A lot of my early memories of teenage years were violence, the sheer fear of leaving the house to catch the bus."[16]

The song was developed by The Edge around a pre-recorded drum loop by Larry. Bono relates "With U2 I sometimes write lyrics, and then we try to find the music to express those lyrics. But most of the time it's about finding a feeling first, and then trying to express that feeling. So, Edge had this big blues riff, powerful and full of rage. It was a natural fit for me to talk about my own rage."[17]

Gavin Friday documents some of the earliest days of both U2 and the Virgin Prunes, and how they would escape the grey world of Ballymun via their friendships in an alternate version of the song which he narrates on the *Innocence + Experience Live in Paris* video.[18] Gavin further expands on the story of Cedarwood Road via a monthly segment on U2 X-Radio called "The Cedarwood Chronicles" where he shares his story and U2's in the 1970s.

An acoustic version of the song was included on deluxe versions of the album. The original mix is part of the *Rock Band 4* video game, while other U2 songs were later made available to download.

"Sleep Like a Baby Tonight"
Lyrics: Bono/Edge
Music: U2
Producer: Danger Mouse

"Sleep Like a Baby Tonight" was in development for some time. A 1996 press photo of the band in studio has a white board with song titles being developed for *Pop*. One of the songs? "She's Gonna Sleep Like a Baby." Leo Pearson is credited on keyboards, a producer that U2 worked with during *All That You Can't Leave Behind*. Eighteen years after fans first saw the song title it was finally released.

Looking back on Dublin in the 1970s, Bono remembered some of the darker elements, saying he "remembered all the violence meted out to women by their husbands, the beatings children experienced from their fathers and how, at that time particularly, priests were sexually abusing young children."[19] It is the latter that lead to the lyrics of this song. The dark lyrics may be why U2 have not performed the song in concert.

An alternate mix of the song by Tchad Blake was featured on the deluxe version of the album.

"This is Where You Can Reach Me Now"
Lyrics: Bono/Edge
Music: U2
Producer: Danger Mouse

Songs of Innocence opens with a look at when the Ramones visited Dublin. This song is about another concert that had a big effect on U2, the Clash in 1977. Bono remembers the show:

Wow that looks like a revolution we want to be a part of, and they keep saying from the stage "this is yours, you own this, it's not us" and we were going oh yeah OK. After the Clash gig we just kind of moved address, we went home, we slept in the same beds, but not really. We had moved address, spiritually so to speak, we'd never be the same again.[20]

Gavin Friday attended that show with Bono and said he walked home with Bono after the show, and they knew what they needed to do—go off and form bands.[21]

Bono compared falling into the music scene as being a different sort of soldier, "Back in 1977 this was a militancy that contrasted with all the shite that was going on in Ireland. All the sort of terrorism. This was indoor terrorism. Here was this other type of soldier."[22]

The song features Larry Mullen on backing vocals.

"THE TROUBLES"

Lyrics: Bono/Edge
Music: U2
Producer: Danger Mouse
Additional: Gaffney

The final song on *Songs of Innocence* takes another look at the dark side of Dublin in the 1970s, this time looking at domestic abuse. Bono remembers "I remember those bullies. The dads brutalizing their kids, the husband brutalizing the wife. I can't stand bullies. I can't stand them online; I can't stand them in front of me. Defining yourself by degrading someone else."[23]

The song features Lykke Li on lead vocals, sharing the duties with Bono. The song, which Bono described as "an uncomfortable song about domestic violence," needed a woman's touch, and Bono felt Li provided the perfect voice. "She puts us all under a spell with her music. We needed a feminine spirit; she was the right one."[24]

The song was performed a handful of times live in concert with Bono singing along with a pre-recorded version of the song by Lykke Li on the video screens. An alternate version of the song also appeared on deluxe versions of the album.

Extras from the Era

"Ordinary Love" appeared a year before *Songs of Innocence* via the soundtrack for *Mandela: Long Walk to Freedom*. It was the first song released from U2's work with Danger Mouse. Backing vocals on the song are by Angel Deradoorian, known for her work with Dirty Projectors. The lyrics discuss the love between Winnie and Nelson Mandela. U2 released the song for the Record Store Day

Black Friday event. Several mixes of the song were made available, with different versions appearing in the film and promotion. Paul Epworth also provided a mix as well. Two videos were developed, a lyric video directed by Oliver Jeffers and Mac Premo using the soundtrack mix, and a video with additional footage of the band set to the Epworth mix. The "Extraordinary Remix" appeared as a bonus track on deluxe versions of *Songs of Experience*.

"Invisible" is a song inspired by U2's first trip to London. Bono told *Rolling Stone*, "There were really wild extraordinary people and then you feel deeply not extraordinary. You feel invisible and you're screaming to be seen."[25] The song was released for charity. The song was made available on iTunes for free for twenty-four hours. For each download of the song, Bank of America pledged to donate $1 to (RED) to help in the fight against AIDS. A total of $3,138,470 (US) was raised for (RED) through this donation, which surpassed the original expected donation of $2,000,000. After the initial download, the song was made available at other stores. The initial version was an edit of the song, the full version was released as a hidden track on *Songs of Innocence*. A video for the song was filmed by Mark Romanek in black-and-white, featuring U2 performing in front of a digital screen behind the band.

Two additional new songs appeared on the deluxe version of *Songs of Innocence*. "The Crystal Ballroom" is named for a dance hall in Dublin where Bono's mother and father used to dance which became McGonagles, a club U2 played in the early days. Debuting the song in Chicago Bono told the crowd, "I thought it was a bit weird we ended up at a punk club where my mother and father used to make out. Something just a little funky about that, in a good way."[26] A longer remix was released as a bonus track on vinyl versions of *Songs of Innocence* and as an extra track on deluxe versions in Japan.

"Lucifer's Hands" was the other new track on deluxe versions of *Songs of Innocence*. The song developed from an instrumental track that U2 played during the U2360° Tour called "Return of the Stingray Guitar." That song title was identified in notebooks documenting *The Unforgettable Fire* album sessions. It has been suggested that The Edge uncovered the old instrumental during work on the twenty-fifth anniversary release of *The Unforgettable Fire* and the band dusted it off for live performances the following year.

15

Songs of Experience
(2017)

Songs of Experience was released on December 1, 2017. Originally the album had been planned for an October 31, 2016 release, but U2 chose to delay the release for a year as they saw the political climate changing in the world and felt the album would benefit from additional work. For the album U2 worked with producers Jacknife Lee, Ryan Tedder and Brent Kutzle (OneRepublic), Andy Barlow (Lamb), Steve Lillywhite, Jolyon Thomas, Paul Epworth, and Declan Gaffney. Recording took place in various studios in New York, California, Ireland, and London. Andy Barlow traveled with U2 while on tour working with a mobile recording studio.

The cover of the album features Bono's son, Eli, holding hands with The Edge's daughter, Sian. Sian is wearing an army helmet, a reference to the helmet Peter Rowen wore in earlier covers. The photograph is by Anton Corbijn and design on the album was by Shaughn McGrath.

The songs on the album were developed as a series of letters to people in Bono's life. The Irish poet Brendan Kennelly had given Bono some advice to write as if he were dead. The letter idea was followed up in promotion of the album. Two postal campaigns were conducted with fans receiving mysterious letters in the mail hinting at song titles and lyrics. Promotional envelopes and writing paper were given out at album listening parties.

The album was listed at #3 on the *Rolling Stone* list of the 50 Best Albums of 2017. The album debuted at #1 in the US charts and #5 in the UK Charts. In the US, the album was bundled with concert tickets, meaning every ticket sold came with a copy of the album, and counted towards chart positions.

"LOVE IS ALL WE HAVE LEFT"
Lyrics: Bono
Music: U2
Producer: Barlow

The album opens with Bono's voice through a vocoder and Bono told *Rolling Stone* that this was his "favourite opening line to a U2 album."[1] Bono first mentioned the song in 2006 calling it an "old Broadway tune, I thought it was a Frank Sinatra song" and later sharing he was "pretending to be Frank Sinatra singing on the moon, a sci-fi torch song."[2, 3] The lyrics link back to "Walk On" covering similar ground. A song called "Love Is" was also in development during the *All That You Can't Leave Behind* sessions.

In Europe for the 2018 tour, the song was remixed with elements of "Zooropa" and Charlie Chaplin's speech from *The Great Dictator*. "The Europa EP," released for Record Store Day featured this live mix on one side, and the B-side featured a remix by Jon Pleased Wimmin who said, "The first time I heard it gave me goosebumps, it was on headphones in the dark on the day of release of *Songs of Experience....* I could hear exactly how I'd remix it straight away and envisaged it as a Space Age Lullaby."[4] Another remix, by long-time collaborator Paul Oakenfold, has not been officially released.

Patti Smith has covered the song in many of her recent performances.

"LIGHTS OF HOME"
Lyrics: Bono
Music: U2/Alana Haim/Danielle Haim/Este Haim/Rechshaid
Producers: Lee, Tedder, Kutzle
Additional: Thomas

Bono shared he had a "brush of mortality" at Christmas 2016, later revealed to be a blister on his aorta, requiring surgery.[5] "Lights of Home" deals with such a topic, but it may not be just Bono's brush with mortality. In early 2014, Irish musician Christy Dignam shared that Bono had been working on a song called "The Light" and that Bono had shared the lyrics when Dignam spoke about his own near-death experience. The lyrics feature a line from "Iris" linking back to *Songs of Innocence*.

The band Haim and producer Ariel Rechtshaid get a co-writing credit, and in July 2016 joined U2 in studio to record backing vocals. The song is built around a bass line in Haim's "Song 5." Haim would later ask if Bono would appear on their song "Summer Girl," but he declined saying his voice was not up to par.

"Lights of Home" was the fourth commercial single from *Songs of Experience*. The single included the St Peter's String Version (also on deluxe versions of the album) and the "Free Yourself Remix" by Beck. The cover art includes an image of Dublin at night taken from the International Space Station on St Patrick's Day 2017. An alternate mix of the song features on a *MOJO* compilation.

"You're the Best Thing About Me"
Lyrics: Bono
Music: U2
Producers: Lee, Tedder, Lillywhite, Kutzle

"You're the Best Thing About Me" is a letter from Bono to his wife, Ali. Each night on tour, Bono would compose letters to Ali at the start of the song as he removed his Macphisto makeup. The title came from Irish writer Eamon Dunphy, who remembers, "We were just out having a drink. It was really nothing serious, but he remembered it—it must have been 10 or 15 years ago. She's a wonderful girl. So that's all I said."[6]

When the album was pushed back a year, word did not get to Kygo, who had remixed the song. He played his remix in a festival appearance in Norway in August 2016 giving fans a preview of the song. The remix included early lines about fresh paint that were dropped from the released version.

When the song debuted, a lyric video was also released featuring a book of lyrics and art containing the song. A promotional release sent to radio stations included a second mix of the song, the Sci-Fi Soul Remix (remixed by Jacknife Lee). Two weeks later, the new remix by Kygo was released commercially and a live performance video was issued showing Kygo spinning his remix.

Four weeks after the initial release, a new video for the song directed by Jonas Åkerlund was released. The video shows U2 enjoying New York City, riding through the streets, enjoying pizza, and driving around in a sightseeing bus. Press releases accompanying the video state, the video "serves as a visual tapestry of tribute to New York and a serenade to the city's iconic symbols of American compassion and liberty."[7] An acoustic version was also issued in audio formats.

A week later, a short film by Tatia Pilieva followed four couples who are in love but forced to be apart, following them as they say goodbye. A sixth video for the song was filmed in Amsterdam featuring a girl dancing on stage with U2, holding up song lyrics in the audience and spray painting them around town has never been released.

To celebrate U2's first performance in India the song was remixed by OX7GEN for an EP of remixes by Indian DJs, titled "The Eternal Remixes."

"Get Out of Your Own Way"
Lyrics: Bono
Music: U2
Producers: Tedder, Lillywhite, Kutzle, Thomas
Additional: Lee

"Get Out of Your Own Way" was a letter to Bono's daughters. It was developed out of demos that had led U2 to "Beautiful Day" and there are some similarities in sound. The song was the third single released.

Two remixes were done, by Switch and Afrojack. Each featured a longer version for promotional purposes and a shorter edit that was commercially released. Additional remixes were planned but U2 switched gears. Will Clarke shared, "When I first got asked to remix U2 I was sent the parts to 'Get Out.' I completed the remix, and everyone was super into it; however, U2's team changed their mind on what needed being remixed so they gave me the parts to 'Love Is Bigger.'"[8] Clarke's remix of "Get Out of Your Own Way" remains unreleased.

A stop-motion video, directed by the Israeli street art collective known as Broken Fingaz, was a political statement, including scenes of the Ku Klux Klan marching past the White House while Trump sat in the Oval Office. Broken Fingaz explained, "The video addresses the current political situation. 2017 for us was the year fascists worldwide felt confident enough to raise their heads again, encouraged by Trump and other world leaders, who use people's fear to build more walls and segregation."[9] The video was also recut to accompany both remixes of the song.

Two other videos were filmed but never used. A video directed by Jonas Åkerlund was filmed on a roof in Mexico City, with U2 performing the song while young people danced around them with coloured smoke. The rooftop was decorated with traditional Mexican elements. *La Reforma* explained these were props from the James Bond film *Spectre*, and U2 had failed to get the permission of the artists to use these materials, leaving the video unused.[10] Another video was filmed during a performance in Trafalgar Square, with U2 performing in front of Nelson's column. Audience members were given protest signs to hold up during the song, but it too did not get released.

"American Soul"
Lyrics: Bono
Music: U2
Produers: Lee
Additional: Thomas, Gaffney

"American Soul" started with "Glastonbury," developed into "Volcano" on *Songs of Innocence* and continued to become "American Soul." It is one of many shared ideas between the two albums. Lyrics from "American Soul" also appear in "XXX" recorded by U2 with Kendrick Lamar, in return, Lamar would appear on *Songs of Experience* in the transition between "Get Out of Your Own Way" and "American Soul." The lines we hear Lamar read between the songs on U2's album are based on the Beatitudes, eight blessings shared by Jesus in the Gospel of Matthew.

Bono has described the final version of "American Soul" as a letter to America. He told WXRT, "it's about how we came to America, there was something of America in rock and roll, but what was it, it was a beautiful racial mix, that was what rock and roll was, gospel and the blues had a bastard child called rock and roll."[11]

A video by Broken Fingaz was the first project they worked on with U2. They were given a week to put the lyric video together, with footage filmed in Israel, India, and the UK. The footage for the lyric video was also used as backing when U2 performed the song on *Saturday Night Live*. A second video followed a few months later, featuring footage of U2 performing on a barge in the Hudson River with the Statue of Liberty in the background. It was mixed with footage created and used in the lyric video by Broken Fingaz. The song was not commercially released, but it was distributed to radio in Europe.

The barge footage was also used in advertisements for the 2018 NCAA March Madness basketball tournament. "American Soul" was the theme song of the tournament. Footage from the barge was also used on the 2018 Grammy Awards as U2 performed "Get Out of Your Own Way"—at that ceremony, Bono and The Edge would also appear live on stage with Kendrick Lamar performing "XXX."

"SUMMER OF LOVE"
Lyrics: Bono
Music: U2
Producers: Tedder, Kutzle
Additional: Lee

"Summer of Love" draws from the war that was ongoing in Syria. A refugee crisis was happening on the Mediterranean, where U2 spend a lot of time in their homes near Eze. Edge shared:

> One of the jumping-off points was a CNN story about the gardener of Aleppo. It's about this guy who ran a garden in Aleppo that he kept going through the entire war. It was a political statement to the entire world that he kept this garden going. He was this deeply philosophical character and to him it was an act of defiance to grow flowers in the middle of Aleppo. He actually wound up getting killed in an air raid, so it was a very sad ending, but Bono was really inspired by his defiance.[12]

Like "Lights of Home," this song had elements taken from another song, an unreleased song at the time by OneRepublic called "West Coast." The song features some of the guitar and other elements of "Summer of Love." "West Coast" by OneRepublic was released in February 2022, and Ryan Tedder calls it a favourite. "Summer of Love" is produced by Ryan Tedder and Brent Kutzle, who also play keyboards and guitar on the track. Backing vocals on the track include Lady Gaga.

"Summer of Love" was the sixth and final single from the album. Two EPs of remixes were released including mixes by Mick Park and Danny Stubbs, Rusty

Egan, Howie B, and more. A total of twenty-six remixes in total were released, pushing "Summer of Love" to #7 on the Dance/Club Songs chart in the US. A planned remix featuring vocals from former Fifth Harmony member Lauren Jauregui has never been released.

"Summer of Love" was one of the songs chosen by actor Matthew McConaughey as a favourite when he hosted his own show on U2 X-Radio on SiriusXM.

"RED FLAG DAY"
Lyrics: Bono
Music: U2
Producer: Tedder, Lillywhite, Kutzle, Barlow

"Red Flag Day" developed from "The Lies That We Believe" which Edge discussed with Dave Fanning. He had joined Larry in the studio who was playing a fun drum beat, "So I walked in and thought OK, I'll try this other song over the beat. It started off, became this pretty cool tune with Danger Mouse but it didn't go on the album, primarily because it turned out it didn't have a kind of vitality."[13] The Edge described the final song as "something from 1978."[14] "Red Flag Day" is one of two songs on the album to reference the refugee crisis in Europe with Bono saying both songs "have a similar theme, about people running for their lives on the same Mediterranean that we're running through the shallows."[15] Backing vocals include the voices of Ryan Tedder and Julian Lennon.

At one point "Red Flag Day" was identified as a possible single from the album, and remixes were commissioned from several DJs which remain unreleased. A video was put together with the World Surf League for the song using surf footage at beaches from South Africa, Portugal, Brazil, and Hawaii. The video aired during the #24HoursOfReality programming organized by Al Gore to address the issue of climate change.

"THE SHOWMAN (LITTLE MORE BETTER)"
Lyrics: Bono
Music: U2
Producers: Tedder, Lillywhite
Additional: Lee

"The Showman (Little More Better)" is a letter to U2's audience. Bono shared that he believed performers cannot be trusted and called the song one of his favourites on the new album as U2 were still recording. An earlier, unreleased version of the song was mentioned in 2015 in Q Magazine, when it was still titled "Much More Better."[16] Descriptions of the song in these early interviews describe it as being an acoustic demo dealing with his accident in 2014.

"The Showman (Little More Better)" has never been performed in concert. In the 2018 rehearsals, it was rehearsed extensively before being abandoned. Bono would work the lyrics into the show speaking lyrics ahead of "You're the Best Thing About Me." It is the only song on the main album which has not been performed live.

Little Steven chose "The Showman (Little More Better)" as one of his favourite U2 tracks when he hosted a segment on U2 X-Radio.

"THE LITTLE THINGS THAT GIVE YOU AWAY"

Lyrics: Bono
Music: U2
Producers: Thomas
Additional: Barlow

"The Little Things That Give You Away" was a letter to Bono himself, but it took Bono to realize who his audience was. He shared, "In all of these advice type songs, you are of course preaching what you need to hear. In that sense, they're all written to the singer."[17]

The song started life as "Lead Me in the Way I Should Go," a song that was developed for *How to Dismantle an Atomic Bomb*. In an interview published in *Grammy Magazine*, Bono claimed the song would be a "big song."[18] The song would get mentioned again in 2014 under the title "The Morning After Innocence." "The Little Things" was first teased by U2 on their social media accounts in June 2015, when Bono posted the lyrics to the song. Bono also shared the lyrics with U2.com in January 2017 although with a few altered lyrics, calling it "my favourite at the moment."[19]

While rehearsing for the 2017 tour in Vancouver, it was noted that U2 continued to practice with the PA off so people outside the stadium would not hear songs clearly. Word spread quickly that it was a new song being worked on. During the first show of that tour, the song was played in full at the end of the night, the first from the new album, and a preview of the cover art was revealed on the screen behind U2.

While promoting the album, an in-studio live performance of the song was shared as a Spotify exclusive.

"LANDLADY"

Lyrics: Bono
Music: U2
Producers: Lee, Tedder
Additional: Barlow

"Landlady" is about Ali, who Bono married in 1982. At times she helped keep Bono afloat, even paying the rent. Bono explained, "I just don't want to write her an obnoxious, sentimental song—she deserves better than that."[20]

The song was not rehearsed for the 2018 tour, and fans stopped U2 frequently to ask for it. Heading into a show in Milan, Bono told one fan he would see what he could do, and the song debuted that night. It was played twice in Milan and one time in Dublin. On the heels of the performances in Milan, Universal in Italy announced they would release the song to radio. It was not released in other countries.

Producer, Jacknife Lee played "Landlady" as one of his favourite U2 songs when guest hosting on U2 X-Radio. Lee appears on the track on additional guitars.

"THE BLACKOUT"
Lyrics: Bono
Producers: Lee, Tedder
Additional: Kutzle

"The Blackout" started life as a discussion of Bono's own mortality, but when the album was delayed, it was reworked after Donald Trump's election to be a more politically inspired song. Although "You're the Best Thing" was the first single released, "The Blackout" was the first video released from the album, in a video directed by Richie Smyth.

The video was filmed in Amsterdam in a small club in front of several fans invited via U2.com. U2 performed the song several times with both Bono and Adam Clayton going into the crowd during the performances. The video aired on Facebook live, and in the first week it was viewed 11.1 million times, placing it at #1 for the *Billboard* Top Facebook Live videos chart. Fans in line for the concert in Amsterdam the next day were heard humming the song, trying to remember the lyrics and melody.

The song was the second commercial single from the album and the first physical release from the album, with a 12-inch vinyl pressing on Third Man Records for Record Store Day's Black Friday event. It was backed with a Jacknife Lee Remix of the song. A limited pressing in black-and-white vinyl was limited to 750 copies sold only at Third Man Records in Detroit and Nashville, Freebird Records in Dublin, and Rough Trade in London. Ten test pressings in black vinyl were also given away by Third Man Records. The release on vinyl reached #2 in the Vinyl Singles chart in the UK and reached #2 in the Physical Singles chart in the UK. An instrumental mix of "The Blackout" was also distributed to radio.

"LOVE IS BIGGER THAN ANYTHING IN ITS WAY"

Lyrics: Bono
Music: U2
Producers: Lee

"Love is Bigger Than Anything in its Way" was Bono "singing to my sons, but I'm singing to myself. The teenage rage, that thing, I really relate to it."[21] The song features keyboards by Andrew Taggart of The Chainsmokers, an American pop group, and additional vocal and guitar by Jacknife Lee.

U2 have shared the song with the LGBTQ community worldwide. A video directed by David Mushegain features LGBTQ youth and their support networks from Dublin, dancing, singing, and enjoying life. Mushegain posted on his Instagram, "It was so awesome to be able to combine two subjects that are very close to my heart, Dublin youth culture and the LGBTQ scene." Promotional tie-ins such as stickers and fans featured a rainbow design to tie into Pride celebrations, and club nights were arranged in gay clubs throughout North America to promote the single. The song was also used in the opening celebration in Paris for the Gay Games in 2018.

Promotion of the song featured a campaign of remixes. Nine different versions of the track were released commercially including two EPs of remixes, an acoustic version of the song and remixes by Cheat Codes and Beck. Several additional remixes promoted the song throughout the summer, including mixes by Offer Nissim, Robbie Rivera, and Daybreakers. The remixes pushed the song to #1 on the Dance/Club Songs chart in the USA (one final remix was completed by Lost Stories in 2019, part of an EP of songs remixed by Indian artists called "The Eternal Remixes").

Broken Fingaz directed two animated videos for the song, one for the Cheat Codes remix and the other for the Beck Remix. The first was traditional animation, with a series of objects moving around the screen. The second was animated models, telling a story of a man who has lost his wife. Several the DJs involved in mixing the song also generated their own videos to accompany the song from the existing ones or using their own images.

A release planned for Record Store Day's Black Friday event in 2018 was a 7-inch single in red vinyl, with "Love is Bigger" on one side and "Red Flag Day" on the other. Both were recorded direct to acetate at Third Man Records in Nashville. In the end, U2 was unhappy with the results and chose not to issue the single after reviewing test pressings.

In concert, the crowd would sing along long after U2 had stopped, and in Montreal after the show, fans could be hearing the ending chant for blocks after leaving the arena.

"13 (There is A Light)"

Lyrics: Bono
Music: U2
Producers: Tedder, Epworth

"13 (There is A Light)" is the thirteenth and final song on the album. The song borrows musically and lyrically from "Song for Someone," written for Bono's wife Ali. "13" is addressed to his kids, with Bono revealing "the idea was to write for the teenage girl that you fell in love with, and then for her children."[22] The song lyrics touch on Bono's brush with mortality.

"13" was one of the first songs finished and it almost appeared on *Songs of Innocence*. The Edge said it "was in the running for the last record, and then at a certain point we had the potential of the two songs. The chorus was common to both. But we thought we would bring 'There Is A Light' into *Songs of Experience* because we liked the idea of there being a bridge."[23] U2 discussed using it as a hidden track, but that is not so easy with streaming services, and thus it was given a name instead.

On tour, "13" was the final song played in 2018 as a large lightbulb rose from a model of Bono's childhood home at 10 Cedarwood. Bono cradles the bulb as he sings. The 2015 concerts had opened with the large lightbulb and "The Miracle (of Joey Ramone)" and the 2018 shows closed the circle, often ending with a remix of "The Miracle (of Joey Ramone)."

Extras from the Era

"Book of Your Heart" featured on deluxe versions of the album. Bono told Bill Flanagan, "I wanted to write about the cold passion of great relationships.... It's about the knowingness that you need to help get your partner through their life, and vice versa."[24]

"XXX" is a song by Kendrick Lamar which credits U2 from his album, *Damn*, released ahead of *Songs of Experience*. On the song Bono sings lyrics that will be later heard as part of "American Soul." The song reached *Billboard*'s Hot 100, meaning U2 had a Top 40 hit in each of the four decades from the 1980s through the 2010s. Only four other artists had done that before them, Michael Jackson, Madonna, Weird Al, and Kenny G.

"Message to Souris" was a strange song released in 2018, featuring Bono leaving an answering machine message to a deceased cat, and reading Rainer Maria Rilke's "The Black Cat" while "An Cat Dubh" played in the background. It was released on a compilation by artist Sophie Calle, dedicated to her cat Souris.

"Ahimsa" was a song U2 developed with A.R. Rahman in advance of their first concert in India. The word is a Sanskrit word for non-violence. Additional vocals in Tamil are sung by Rahman's daughters Khatija and Raheema, singing lines from Chapter 32 of *Tirukkural*, a piece of early Tamil literature. A.R. Rahman can be heard on the final chorus. Two lyric videos were released, with the first being quickly removed from streaming services and replaced with the second, which uses animated versions of Bono's lyrics. A remix by KSHMR was also released.

"Your Song Saved My Life" was released in 2021 as part of the film *Sing 2*. Bono voices a character of an aged lion in the film who has retired from life as a rock star on the loss of his wife. He is coaxed back to performing by the other characters in the film. Various edits of the song were released to promotional services, one adding extra lyrics not featured in the soundtrack version. The song was nominated for Original Song from an Animated Film at the Hollywood Music in Media Awards but did not win the award. And although it made the shortlist of ten songs for Original Song at the 2022 Oscars, it did make the final cut to be one of the songs nominated for the award.

A lyric video using Bono's animated lyrics was done, followed by a video directed by Aya Tanimura, featuring children using music to improve their lives through the Education Through Music program. Bono told *Variety*, "I'd made notes earlier, over the years, on this idea of: Some people sing for a living, some people sing to stay alive.... There are all kinds of reasons people sing, And I've had this in my head. But only when I got this character, Clay Calloway, did I think, 'Okay, this is the guy who can talk about it, and I can use this vehicle of this character.'"[25] The song "Calloway Says No" on the score for the film makes use of the melodies from "Your Song Saved My Life" and writing is partially credited to U2 as well.

In 2023, U2 released *Songs of Surrender*, remaking forty of their classic songs. U2 were the first performers at the Sphere in Las Vegas, releasing "Atomic City" to celebrate the twenty-five shows. The song title is a name given to the city by the Chamber of Commerce in the 1940s. Lyrics include luck, dice, roulette, and name check Frank Sinatra. Bono shares that Blondie and The Clash inspired the music. A new album is expected soon.

U2 Covering Other Artists' Songs

U2 have covered several songs by other artists, including these on compilations and as B-sides. Below is a list of officially released covers, followed by the original artist performing the song, and then the first U2 release of the song.

"Ave Maria" (Traditional) ["Sometimes You Can't Make it On Your Own" Single, 2005, Performed with Pavarotti]

"Bang A Gong (Get It On)" (T. Rex) [*AngelHeaded Hipster: The Songs of Marc Bolan & T.Rex* Album, 2020, Performed with Elton John]

"Beat on the Brat" (The Ramones) [*We're A Happy Family* Album, 2003]

"Can't Help Falling in Love" (Elvis Presley) ["Who's Gonna Ride Your Wild Horses" Single, 1992]

"Christmas (Baby, Please Come Home)" (Darlene Love) [*A Very Special Christmas* Album, 1987]

"Dancing Barefoot" (Patti Smith) ["When Love Comes to Town" Single, 1989]

"Don't Take Your Guns to Town" (Johnny Cash) ["Elevation" Single, 2001]

"Everlasting Love" (Robert Knight) ["All I Want is You" Single, 1989]

"Everybody Loves A Winner Baby" (William Bell) [*Achtung Baby* 20th Anniversary Collection, 2011]

"Fortunate Son" (Creedence Clearwater Revival) ["Who's Gonna Ride Your Wild Horses" Single, 1992]

"Happiness is a Warm Gun" (The Beatles) ["Last Night on Earth" Single, 1997]

"I Believe in Father Christmas" (Greg Lake) [*(RED)Wire* Digital Magazine, 2008]

"Instant Karma" (John Lennon and the Plastic Ono Band) [*Instant Karma: The Campaign to Save Darfur* Album, 2007]

"Jesus Christ" (Woodie Guthrie) [*Folkways: A Vision Shared* Album, 1988]

"Neon Lights" (Kraftwerk) ["Vertigo" Single, 2004]

"Night and Day" (Cole Porter, performed by Fred Astaire) [*Red, Hot and Blue* Album, 1990]

"Paint it Black" (Rolling Stones) ["Who's Gonna Ride Your Wild Horses" Single, 1992]

"Pop Muzik" (M) ["Last Night on Earth" Single, 1997]

"The Saints Are Coming" (The Skids) ["The Saints Are Coming" Single, 2006, Performed with Green Day]

"Satellite of Love" (Lou Reed) ["One" Single, 1992]

"Tower of Song" (Leonard Cohen) [*Leonard Cohen: I'm Your Man* Album, 2006, Performed with Leonard Cohen]

"Unchained Melody" (Todd Duncan) ["All I Want is You" Single, 1989]

"What's Going On?" (Marvin Gaye) ["Spotify Singles" Single, 2017]

U2 have also released several live covers of songs from other artists, below is a list of some of these covers where the full song was performed.

"All Along the Watchtower" (Bob Dylan) [*Rattle and Hum* Album, 1988]

"Amazing Grace" (Traditional) [*U2360° at the Rose Bowl* Video, 2010]

"The Auld Triangle" (Dick Shannon) [*The Late Late Show Tribute to the Dubliners* Album, 2008, Performed with full cast]

"Because the Night" (Bruce Springsteen) [*The 25th Anniversary Rock & Roll Hall of Fame Concerts* Album, 2010, Performed with Patti Smith, Bruce Springsteen]

"Gimme Shelter" (Rolling Stones) [*The 25th Anniversary Rock & Roll Hall of Fame Concerts* Album, 2010, Performed with Mick Jagger]

"Helter Skelter" (The Beatles) [*Rattle and Hum* Album, 1988]

"Help!" (The Beatles) [*¡Released! The Human Rights Concerts* Album, 2013]

"I Remember You" (The Ramones) ["Elevation" Single, 2001]

"Maggie's Farm" (Bob Dylan) [*Self Aid* Album, 1987]

"People Have the Power" (Patti Smith) [*Innocence + Experience Live in Paris* Video, 2016, Performed with Patti Smith]

"Sgt. Pepper's Lonely Hearts Club Band" (The Beatles) ["Live 8: One Day One Concert One World" Single, 2005, Performed with Paul McCartney]

"Springhill Mining Disaster" (Ewan MacColl / Peggy Seeger) (a.k.a. "The Ballad of Springhill") [*The Late Late Show Tribute to the Dubliners* Album, 2008]

"Where Is the Love?" (Black Eyed Peas) [*The 25th Anniversary Rock & Roll Hall of Fame Concerts* Album, 2010, Performed with the Black Eyed Peas]

"I've Got You Under My Skin" has also been released on U2's "Stay (Faraway, So Close!)" single, but is credited to Bono and Frank Sinatra, and not to U2. Likewise, an earlier recording of "Can't Help Falling in Love" is credited to Bono on the soundtrack to *Honeymoon in Vegas*, we've listed the first band credited version above instead.

U2 Solo Works

Adam Clayton Solo Work

1984 Band Aid: "Do They Know it's Christmas/Feed the World"
1989 Daniel Lanois: "Jolie Louise/Still Water"
1991 The Hughes' Band: "The Bucks of Oranmore"
1991 Sharon Shannon: "The Marguerita Suite"
1994 Nanci Griffith: "These Days in an Open Book/Don't Forget About Me/On Grafton Street"
1995 Automatic Baby: "One"
1996 Bono and Adam Clayton: "Tomorrow"
1996 Adam Clayton and Larry Mullen: "Theme from Mission: Impossible" and "Mission: Impossible Theme" and various mixes
1999 Little Steven: *Born Again Savage* Album (Adam plays bass on entire album)
2000 Tito Larriva and the MDH Band: "Anarchy in the USA"
2004 Nancy Sinatra: "Two Shots of Happy, One Shot of Sad"
2019 Sharon Shannon: "Larry O'gaff's Set"
2021 Kristel: "Take it Easy"

Bono Solo Work

1984 Band Aid: "Do They Know it's Christmas/Feed the World"
1985 Clannad: "In a Lifetime"
1985 Artists United Against Apartheid: "Sun City/Silver and Gold"
1987 T-Bone Burnett: "Purple Heart"
1989 Roy Orbison: "She's a Mystery to Me"
1989 Melissa Etheridge: "Royal Station 4/16"
1990 Ecco Homo: "New York New York" and various mixes
1990 The Call: "What's Happened to You"
1992 Bono: "Can't Help Falling in Love"
1993 Frank Sinatra with Bono: "I've Got You Under My Skin"
1994 Bono and Gavin Friday: "In the Name of the Father/Billy Boola"
1994 The Chieftains: "The Long Black Veil"
1995 Christy Moore with Bono and The Edge: "North & South of the River"
1995 Bono: "Hallelujah"
1995 Gavin Friday: "Little Black Dress"
1995 Bono: "Save the Children"
1996 Passengers: "Miss Sarajevo/One" (Live from Modena)

1996 Pavarotti and Friends: "Nessun Dorma" (Live from Modena)
1996 Carl Perkins and Friends: "Give Me Back My Job"
1997 Bono and Larry Mullen: "Dreaming with Tears in My Eyes"
1997 Various Artists: "Perfect Day '97"
1998 Bono: "Mothers of the Disappeared/Mother of God"
1998 Kirk Franklin: "Lean on Me"
1999 David A. Stewart: "A Good Man"
1999 Lone Justice: "Sweet Jane" (Live from Hartford)
1999 Wyclef Jean featuring Bono: "New Day" (and various mixes)
1999 Micheal Hutchence: "Slide Away"
2000 Various: *Million Dollar Hotel* Soundtrack (Bono executive produces and performs on several tracks)
2000 Mocean Worker: "Air Suspension"
2001 Bono and Gavin Friday: "Children of the Revolution"
2001 Mick Jagger: "Joy"
2001 Andrea Bocelli: "L'Incontro" (English Version)
2001 Artists Against AIDS Worldwide: "What's Going On?" (And various Mixes)
2001 The Corrs with Bono: "When the Stars Go Blue/Summer Wine"
2001 Craig Armstrong with Bono: "Stay (Faraway, So Close!)"
2002 Bono: "Anthem"
2002 Bono with Jools Holland and His Rhythm & Blues Orchestra: "If You Wear that Velvet Dress"
2003 Daniel Lanois and Bono: "Falling at Your Feet"
2003 Bono: "That's Life"
2003 Bono, David Stewart, Youssou N'Dour: "46664"
2003 Bono: "God's Laughter"
2004 Various: "American Prayer/46664/Amandla/One/Unchained Melody/46664 Chant" (Live from Cape Town)
2004 Simple Minds: "New Gold Dream (81, 82, 83, 84)"
2005 Various: "Across the Universe" (Live from Los Angeles)
2007 Stevie Wonder and Bono: "Loves is in Need of Love of Love Today"
2007 Pearl Jam featuring Bono and The Edge: "Rockin' in the Free World" (Live)
2008 Tom Jones with Bono and The Edge: "Sugar Daddy"
2008 will.i.am, David Foster, Bono, Mary J. Blige, Faith Hill, Seal: "America's Song"
2009 Rocky Dawuni, Bono, Bob Marley and Others: "War/No More Trouble"
2010 Bono and The Edge: "What's Going On?" Reprise
2010 Jay-Z, Rihanna, Bono and The Edge: "Stranded" (Live and Studio Versions)
2010 Angelique Kidjo with Bono and John Legend: "Move On Up"
2011 Paul McCartney and the Rock Hall Jam Band: "Let it Be"
2011 Various: *Spider-Man Turn off the Dark* Album: Bono is involved in all songs as executive producer and appears on vocals on "Rise Above 1/Picture This/A Freak Like Me Needs Company"
2011 Jonathan Ellis and Various (Including Bono): "Path to Zero"
2011 Bono, The I-Threes, Ziggy Marley and the Rock Hall Jam Band: "One Love"
2011 Paul McCartney and the Rock Hall Jam Band (including Bono): "Let it Be"
2012 Bono and The Edge: "Original of the Species" (Acoustic Version)
2012 Grönemeyer featuring Bono: "Mensch"
2012 K'Naan featuring Bono: "Bulletproof Pride"
2012 The Police featuring Bono: "Invisible Sun" (Live)
2012 The Conspirators: "I Shall Be Released" (Live)
2014 Band Aid 30: "Do They Know It's Christmas?" (2014 Version)
2015 Various including Bono: "Strong Girl" (Remix)
2016 Bruce Springsteen with Bono: "Because the Night" (Live)
2016 Bono featuring Grönemeyer: "Stuck in a Moment You Can't Get Out Of" (Live)
2016 The Chainsmokers (with Bono intro): "Honest"
2018 Bono: "September 1913/On Being Asked for a War Poem/Mad as the Mist and Snow"

2018 Street Lights (Including Bono): "Homeward Bound"
2019 Pavarotti and Bono: "Ave Maria" (Live)
2020 Noel Gallagher (with Bono): "Blue Moon Rising"
2020 Bono, Pavarotti, Zucchero: "Miserere" (Live)
2021 Linda Perry and Bono: "Eden (To Find Love)"
2021 Martin Garrix ft Bono and The Edge: "We Are the People"
2021 DMX ft. Bono: "Skyscrapers"
2021 Zucchero ft. Bono: "Canta La Vita (Let Your Love Be Known)"
2021 Bono with Scarlett Johannson: "I Still Haven't Found What I'm Looking For"
2022 Confidence Man ft. Bono and The Edge: "Feels Like a Different Thing"
2022 Bono: "On Raglan Road"
2022 Bono: "Running to Stand Still" (Live from Dublin)

Larry Mullen Solo Work

1986 Paul Brady: "Airwaves"
1986 Christy Moore, Paul Doran, and the Self Aid Band: "Make it Work"
1986 The Edge with Sinéad O'Connor: "Heroine"
1986 Daniel Lanois: "Jolie Louise/Still Water"
1994 Nanci Griffith: "These Days in an Open Book/Don't Forget About Me/On Grafton Street/This Heart"
1994 Automatic Baby: "One" (Live)
1995 Emmylou Harris: "Goodbye/All My Tears/Wrecking Ball/Deeper Well/Every Grain of Sand/Sweet Old World/May This Be Love/Orphan Girl/Waltz Across Texas Tonight"
1996 Larry Mullen and Adam Clayton: "Theme from Mission: Impossible/Mission: Impossible Theme"
1997 Bono (with Larry Mullen): "Dreaming with Tears In My Eyes"
2000 Tito Larriva and the Million Dollar Hotel Band: "Anarchy in the USA"
2004 Nancy Sinatra: "Two Shots of Happy, One Shot of Sad"
2007 Underworld: "Boy, Boy, Boy"
2011 Larry Mullen and Simon Climie: "The Man on the Train Theme"
2014 Emmylou Harris: "Still Water," "Where Will I Be," "Gold"
2017 Alice Cooper: "Paranormal/Dead Flies/Fireball/Paranoiac Personality/Fallen in Love/Dynamite Road/Private Public Breakdown/Holy Water/The Sound of A"
2021 Alice Cooper: "Shut Up and Rock"

The Edge Solo Work

1979 The Teen Commandments: "Something's Better Than Nothing"
1981 The Teen Commandments: "My Baby Left Me"
1983 Jah Wobble, The Edge, Holger Czukay: "Snake Charmer/Hold on to Your Dreams/Snake Charmer" (Reprise)
1986 The Edge: *Captive* Soundtrack
1989 The Prunes: "In the Night"
1990 Ecco Homo: "New York New York"
1991 Donal Lunny and Friends: "April the Third"
1992 Ron Wood: "Somebody Else Might/Ain't Rock and Roll/Show Me"
1995 Christy Moore with Bono and The Edge: "North & South of the River"
1995 Gavin Friday: "Little Black Dress"
1995 Tina Turner: "GoldenEye"
1996 Passengers: "Miss Sarajevo/One" (Live from Modena)
1996 Various Artists: "Nessun Dorma" (Live from Modena)
1996 Russell Mills/Undark: *Undark 3396* Full Album
1999 David A. Stewart: "Patrol Car Blues"

1999 Christy Moore: "What's the Story Git?"
2001 Artists Against AIDS: "What's Going On?" (The London Version)
2003 Wyclef Jean: "Class Reunion"
2004 Various: "American Prayer/46664/Amandla/One/Unchained Melody/46664 Chant" (Live from Cape Town)
2004 The Edge: "The Batman Theme"
2007 Pearl Jam featuring Bono and The Edge: "Rockin' in the Free World" (Live)
2007 Bono and The Edge: "Lucy in the Sky with Diamonds"
2008 Tom Jones with Bono and The Edge: "Sugar Daddy"
2010 Jay-Z, Rihanna, Bono, and The Edge: "Stranded" (Live and Studio Versions)
2010 Stevie Wonder, Dave Stewart, and others: "With You I'm Born Again/Unchained Melody"
2011 Various: *Spider-Man Turn off the Dark* Album: The Edge is involved in all songs as executive producer, and is listed on additional guitars on the album, and appears on vocals on "Rise Above 1/Picture This/Sinistereo/A Freak Like Me Needs Company"
2011 The Rock Hall Jam Band: "All Along the Watchtower/Big River/Shout/Soul Man"
2012 Bono and The Edge: "Original of the Species" (Acoustic Version)
2012 The Edge and Paul Chavez: *Cold Dream Colour* Soundtrack (The Edge is involved in all tracks)
2020 5 Seconds of Summer: "Best Years"
2021 Martin Garrix featuring Bono and The Edge: "We Are the People"
2022 Confidence Man ft. Bono and The Edge: "Feels Like a Different Thing"

U2 Producing/Writing for Others

1983 Fear of Falling: "Prodigal" (Bono produces)
1984 T-Bone Burnett: "Having A Wonderful Time Wish You Were Here" (Bono co-wrote)
1985 Cactus World News: "The Bridge" Single (Bono produces)
1986 Operating Theatre: "Queen of No Heart" Single (Bono produces)
1986 Geoffrey's First Affair: "Midnight Blues" (Larry produces)
1987 Blue in Heaven: "On and On" (The Edge produces)
1990 The Neville Brothers: "Jah Love" (Bono co-wrote)
1990 Republic of Ireland Football Squad: "Put 'em Under Pressure" (Larry produces)
1992 T-Bone Burnett: "I Can Explain Everything (Bono co-writes, uncredited)
1992 Zucchero and Pavarotti: "Miserere" (Bono co-wrote)
1993 Annie Ross and the Low Note Quartet: "Conversation on a Barstool" (Bono and Edge wrote)
1994 Sinéad O'Connor: "You Made Me the Thief of Your Heart/The Father and His Wife the Spirit (Bono co-wrote)
1995 Ronnie Drew: "Drinkin' in the Day" (Bono co-writes)
1995 Hazel O'Connor: "Conversation on a Barstool" (Bono and Edge wrote)
1995 Tina Turner: "GoldenEye" (Bono and Edge write, and executive produce)
1996 Soma: "Love from a Short Distance" (Bono wrote)
1998 Zucchero: "Blue" (Bono writes English Lyrics)
1998 R.E.M.: "Walk Unafraid" (Bono inspires lyrics, uncredited)
2003 Andrea Corr: "Time Enough for Tears" (Bono co-writes)
2004 Nancy Sinatra: "Two Shots of Happy, One Shot of Sad" (Bono and The Edge Co-Write)
2004 The Neville Brothers: "Kingdom Come" (Bono co-writes)
2007 Johnny Hallyday: "I Am the Blues" (Bono co-writes)
2010 Zucchero: "Someone Else's Tears" (Bono co-writes)
2016 Zucchero: "Streets of Surrender (S.O.S.)" (Bono co-writes)

Select Discography

Additional Commercial Albums

1983 *Under a Blood Red Sky* (Live Album)
1998 *The Best of 1980–1990* (Compilation and B-sides Collection)
2002 *The Best of 1990–2000* (Compilation and B-sides Collection)
2006 *U218 Singles* (Compilation Album)
2010 *Artificial Horizon* (Remix Compilation)
2023 *Songs of Surrender* (Compilation of Reimagined U2 Songs)

Fan Club Albums

1995 *Melon* (Fan Club Compilation Album)
2000 *Hasta La Vista Baby* (Live Album)
2006 *U2.Communication* (Live Album)
2007 *Zoo TV Live* (Live Album)
2008 *U2 Go Home: Live from Slane Castle* (Live Album)
2009 *Medium, Rare and Remastered* (Compilation Album)
2010 *Artificial Horizon* (Compilation Album)
2011 *Duals* (Compilation Album)
2012 *U22* (Live Album)
2013 *From the Ground Up: Edge's Picks* (Live Album)
2015 *Another Time Another Place* (Live Album)
2019 *Live Songs of Innocence + Experience* (Live Album)
2021 *Live at the Apollo For One Night Only* (Live Album)
2022 *Achtung Baby 30 Live* (Live Album)

Singles and EPs

1979-09: "Three" (Also 2019-11)
1980-02: "Another Day"
1980-05: "11 O'Clock Tick Tock" (Also 2020-08)
1980-08: "A Day Without Me"
1980-10: "I Will Follow" (Also 1982-08, 1983-12, 2011-06)
1981-07: "Fire" (Also 2021-06)
1981-10: "Gloria" (Also 2021-11)
1982-03: "A Celebration" (Also 2022-04)

1983-05: "For You"
1983-01: "New Year's Day"
1983-03: "Two Hearts Beat as One"
1983-03: "Sunday Bloody Sunday"
1983-08: "40"
1984-09: "Pride (In the Name of Love)"
1985-04: "The Unforgettable Fire"
1985-05: "Wide Awake in America" (Also 2017-05)
1985-05: "Bad"
1987-03: "With or Without You"
1987-05: "I Still Haven't Found What I'm Looking For"
1987-08: "Where the Streets Have No Name"
1987-11: "In God's Country"
1988-03: "One Tree Hill"
1988-09: "Desire"
1988-12: "Angel of Harlem"
1989-04: "When Love Comes to Town"
1989-06: "All I Want is You"
1990: "Island Treasures"
1991-10: "The Fly"
1991-12: "Mysterious Ways"
1992-02: "One"
1992-06: "Even Better Than the Real Thing"
1992-11: "Who's Gonna Ride Your Wild Horses"
1993-08: "Numb"
1993-11: "Lemon"
1993-11: "Stay (Faraway, So Close!)/I've Got You Under My Skin"
1995-06: "Hold Me, Thrill Me, Kiss Me, Kill Me" (Also 2018-11, with Gavin Friday)
1995-11: "Miss Sarajevo" (Passengers)
1997-02: "Discotheque"
1997-04: "Staring at the Sun"
1997-07: "Last Night on Earth"
1997-09: "Please"
1997-09: "PopHeart EP"
1997-12: "If God Will Send His Angels"
1997-12: "Mofo"
1998-10: "Sweetest Thing"
2000-10: "Beautiful Day"
2001-01: "Stuck in a Moment You Can't Get Out Of" (Also 2001-10)
2001-02: "Walk On" (Also 2001-11)
2001-06: "Elevation"
2002-01: "7 (Rare and Remixed)"
2002-10: "Electrical Storm"
2003-04: "Exclusive: Stuck in a Moment Acoustic"
2004-11: "Vertigo"
2004-12: "Live from Under the Brooklyn Bridge"
2005-02: "Sometimes You Can't Make It On Your Own"
2005-02: "All Because of You" (Also 2005-10)
2005-06: "City of Blinding Lights"
2006-01: "Original of the Species"
2006-04: "One" (With Mary J. Blige)
2006-11: "The Saints are Coming" (With Green Day)
2007-01: "Window in the Skies"
2008-02: "The Ballad of Ronnie Drew" (With The Dubliners, Kila, A Band of Bowsies)
2009-01: "Get on Your Boots"
2009-05: "Magnificent"

2009-08: "I'll Go Crazy if I Don't Go Crazy Tonight"
2010-11: "Wide Awake in Europe"
2013-11: "Ordinary Love"
2014-02: "Invisible"
2014-09: "The Miracle (of Joey Ramone)"
2015-02: "Every Breaking Wave"
2015-09: "Song for Someone"
2017-04: "Red Hill Mining Town"
2017-09: "You're the Best Thing About Me"
2017-11: "The Blackout"
2017-12: "Get Out of Your Own Way"
2018-04: "Lights of Home"
2018-05: "Love is Bigger Than Anything in its Way"
2018-08: "Summer of Love"
2019-04: "The Europa EP"
2019-11: "Ahimsa" (With A.R. Rahman)
2019-12: "The Eternal Remixes" EP
2020-11: "Trilogy" EP
2021-03: "The Virtual Road: U2 Go Home: Live from Slane Castle" EP
2021-03: "The Virtual Road: U2 Live at Red Rocks Under a Blood Red Sky" EP
2021-04: "The Virtual Road: PopMart Live from Mexico City" EP
2021-04: "The Virtual Road: Innocence + Experience: Live in Paris" EP
2021-11: "Your Song Saved My Life"
2021-11: "I Believe in Father Christmas"

Endnotes

Chapter 1

1   Breskin, "U2's Passionate Voice," *Rolling Stone*, 8 October 1987, p. 44.
2   U2, *Innocence + Experience Tour*, May 26, 2015, United Center, Chicago, IL.
3   U2Songs.com, "I Will Follow Video," retrieved December 17. 2021.
4   Lozaw, "Love, Devotion & Surrender," *U2 Magazine*, No. 11, June 1984, p. 5.
5   Bono, "Remembering the Marquee," *Another Time, Another Place*, 2015.
6   Gardner, "U2's First Tour," *U2 Magazine*, November 1982, No. 5, p. 4.
7   Stokes, "Boys in Control," *U2 In the Name of Love: A History from Ireland's Hot Press Magazine* (1985), p. 24.
8   Needs, "The Unforgettable Band: A U2 Overview," *Creem Collectors Series*, August 1987, p. 8.
9   McCormick, "Growing Up in Public," *U2 In the Name of Love: A History from Ireland's Hot Press Magazine* (1985), p. 52.
10 U2, *Experience + Innocence Tour*, May 23, 2018, United Center, Chicago, IL.
11 Cook, "A Dreamboat Named Desire," *NME*, February 27, 1982, p. 28.
12 Storey, "A Day Without Me" Press Release, Island Records, October 16, 1980, p. 1.
13 Carty, "Steve Lillywhite: The Man They Call The Closer" *Hot Press*, November 18, 2020, p. 31.
14 Bono, "Remembering the Marquee," *Another Time, Another Place*, 2015.
15 Sams, "Boy at 40: Edge and Adam Clayton," U2Songs.com, December 13, 2020.

Chapter 2

1   Parkyn, "On 'October'," *U2 Magazine*, No. 2, p. 6.
2   Bono and The Edge, interviewed by Phil Sutcliffe, BBC Radio, October 12, 1981.
3   Waters, *Race of Angels: The Genesis of U2* (1994), p. 148.
4   McCormick, *U2 by U2* (2009), p. 148.
5   Bono and The Edge, interviewed by Phil Sutcliffe, BBC Radio, October 12, 1981.
6   Pareles, "A Lyrical Response to a World on Fire," *The New York Times*, September 6, 2017, p. 109.
7   The Edge, *October* Liner Notes, 2008.
8   Carty, "Steve Lillywhite: The Man They Call The Closer" *Hot Press*, November 18, 2020, p. 33.
9   Larry Mullen, BBC Radio, October 6, 1981.
10 Bono and The Edge, interviewed by Phil Sutcliffe, BBC Radio, October 12, 1981.
11 McCormick, *op. cit.*, p. 153.
12 Bono and The Edge, interviewed by Phil Sutcliffe, BBC Radio, October 12, 1981.
13 *Ibid.*
14 Parkyn, "On 'October'," *U2 Magazine*, No. 2, p. 6.
15 McCormick, *op. cit.*, p. 154.

Chapter 3

1 Thrills, "We Went to Bring," *History of Rock 1983*, January 2017, p. 15.
2 *Ibid.*
3 Bono and The Edge, interviewed by Kid Jensen, BBC Radio 1, February 21, 1983.
4 *Ibid.*
5 Stokes, *U2: Into the Heart* (2002), p. 43.
6 Bono and The Edge, interviewed by Kid Jensen, BBC Radio 1, February 21, 1983.
7 U2, NRJ Radio, February 23, 2009.
8 Stokes, *U2: Into the Heart* (2002), p. 43.
9 Thrills, *op. cit.*, p. 15.
10 "U2's producer reveals studio secrets, BBC Website, July 18, 2008, news.bbc.co.uk/2/hi/entertainment/7511370.stm.
11 McCormick, *U2 by U2* (2009), p. 167.
12 Bono, Interviewed by Kid Jensen, BBC Radio 1, January 31, 1983.
13 Bono and The Edge, interviewed by Kid Jensen, BBC Radio 1, February 21 1983.
14 *Ibid.*
15 *Ibid.*

Chapter 4

1 Martin, "We Build the Positive," *History of Rock 1984*, April 2017, p. 133.
2 Adam Clayton and The Edge, interviewed by Tony Michaelides, Piccadilly Radio, December 31, 1984.
3 Martin, *op. cit.*, p. 132.
4 U2, Interviewed by Dave Fanning, RTÉ Radio 2, June 20, 1985.
5 Martin, *op. cit.*, p. 132.
6 Adam Clayton and The Edge, interviewed by Tony Michaelides, Piccadilly Radio, December 31, 1984.
7 U2, Interviewed by Dave Fanning, RTÉ Radio 2, June 20, 1985.
8 Adam Clayton and The Edge, interviewed by Tony Michaelides, Piccadilly Radio, 31 December 1984.
9 Flanagan, "Soul Revelation and The Baptism Of Fire," *Musician*, February 1985, p. 37.
10 Parkyn, "4th of July Explanation," *U2 Magazine*, Summer 1985, No. 15, p. 12.
11 U2, Interviewed by Geno Mitchelini, *Rockline Radio*, 17 December 1984.
12 Adam Clayton and The Edge, interviewed by Tony Michaelides, Piccadilly Radio, December 31, 1984.
13 Hilburn, "U2's Pride (In the Name of Songs): Bono and Edge evaluate one critic's choices for the group's 10 best recordings, from 'I Will Follow' to 'One'," *Los Angeles Times*, September 12, 1993, www.latimes.com/archives/la-xpm-1993-09-12-ca-34478-story.html.
14 Mackey, "The Homecoming," *U2 In the Name of Love: A History from Ireland's Hot Press Magazine* (1985), p. 136.
15 *Ibid.*, p. 136.
16 *Ibid.*, p. 131.
17 *Ibid.*, p. 136.
18 Watson, "In the Name of Love: King's Legacy Lives On," *The Daily Journal*, January 24, 2004, www.atu2.com/news/in-the-name-of-love-kings-legacy-lives-on.html.

Chapter 5

1 Rosenbluth, "Island Mounts All-Out Promo for U2," *Billboard*, March 28, 1987, p. 22.
2 Wroe. "The Joshua Tree," *Propaganda*, 1987, No. 5, p. 11.
3 Hilburn, "Where craft ends and spirit begins," *Los Angeles Times*, August 8, 2004, p. E40.
4 Jennings, "From street punks to rock idealists," *Maclean's*, November 2, 1987, p. 63.

5   Bono, interviewed by Timothy White, "Timothy White's Rock Stars," *Radio Today*, July 13, 1987.

6   Light, "Band of the Year: Rock's Unbreakable Heart" *Spin*, January 2002, p. 58.

7   "Bono Tells Story of U2's 'Bullet the Blue Sky'" Rock & Roll Hall of Fame, May 18 2006, www.youtube.com/watch?v=bPoEn01C4-Q.

8   *Ibid.*

9   Hilburn, "U2's Pride (In the Name of Songs): Bono and Edge evaluate one critic's choices for the group's 10 best recordings, from 'I Will Follow' to 'One'," *Los Angeles Times*, September 12, 1993, www.latimes.com/archives/la-xpm-1993-09-12-ca-34478-story.html.

10 Diehl, "The Making of U2's The Joshua Tree," *Rolling Stone*, May 15, 1997.

11 Hilburn, "U2's Pride (In the Name of Songs)," *op. cit.*

12 Sams, "War Child Presents Heroes," U2Songs.com, retrieved 17 December 2021. (www.u2songs.com/discography/various_artists_war_child_presents_heroes_album).

13 Thrills, "Cactus World View," *New Musical Express*, 14 March 1987. p.25.

14 Bono, interviewed by Timothy White, "Timothy White's Rock Stars," *Radio Today*, July 13, 1987.

15 Stokes, "The World About Us," *Three Chords and the Truth* (1989), p.73.

16 Stokes and Graham, "U2 Give Themselves Away," *Musician*, May 1987, p. 84.

17 U2, *The Old Grey Whistle Test*, March 8, 1987, Balmoral TV Studios, Belfast, Northern Ireland.

18 Wroe. "The Enduring Chill - Bono & the Two Americas," *Propaganda*, 1987, No. 4, p. 6.

19 *Ibid.*

Chapter 6

1   U2, interviewed by Dave Fanning and Timothy White, RTÉ 2FM, October 28, 1988.

2   *Ibid.*

3   U2, interviewed by Roger Scott and Annie Nightingale, BBC Radio 1, October 30, 1988.

4   *Ibid.*

5   McCormick, *U2 by U2* (2009), p. 254.

6   U2, interviewed by Dave Fanning and Timothy White, RTÉ 2FM, October 28, 1988.

7   U2, interviewed by Roger Scott and Annie Nightingale, BBC Radio 1, October 30, 1988.

8   Pond, "U2: Now What?," *Rolling Stone*, May 9, 1989, www.rollingstone.com/music/music-news/u2-now-what-52520/.

9   U2, interviewed by Dave Fanning and Timothy White, RTÉ 2FM, October 28, 1988.

10 *Ibid.*

11 *Ibid.*

12 McCormick, *op. cit.*, p. 257.

13 U2, interviewed by Dave Fanning and Timothy White, RTÉ 2FM, October 28, 1988.

14 McCormick, *op. cit.*, p. 258.

15 U2, interviewed by Roger Scott and Annie Nightingale, BBC Radio 1, October 30, 1988.

Chapter 7

1   Connal, "Exclusive Interview: The Edge," *Hit Parader Presents U2*, June 1992, p. 49.

2   Anton Corbijn, interviewed by John Kelly, "Elevation," U2 X-Radio, November 14, 2021.

3   McCormick, *U2 by U2* (2009), p. 278.

4   Deevoy, "God is in the house" *GQ* magazine, September 3, 2001, www.gq-magazine.co.uk/article/u2-interview-band-of-the-year-2001.

5   "1001 Best Songs Ever," *Q* magazine special edition, 2003.

6   "Close to the Edge," U2 X-Radio, July 1, 2020.

7   Anton Corbijn, interviewed by John Kelly, "Elevation," U2 X-Radio, November 14, 2021.

8   Sams, "One (Version 1 - Director Cut)" U2Songs.com," retrieved December 17, 2021, www.u2songs.com/videos/one_version_1_director_cut.

9   "Close to the Edge," U2 X-Radio, July 1, 2020.

10 Deevoy, "God is in the house" *GQ* magazine, September 3, 2001, www.gq-magazine. co.uk/article/u2-interview-band-of-the-year-2001.
11 Flanagan, "The View from the Edge," *Musician*, March 1992, p. 63.
12 Bailie, "Rock and Roll Should Be This Big!," *NME Originals U2*, November 2002, p. 115.
13 Doyle, "10 Years of Turmoil Inside U2," *Q* magazine, October 2002, p. 86.
14 McCormick, *op. cit.*, p. 282.
15 Wroe, "Achtung Baby Scrapbook," *Propaganda*, 1991, No. 15, p. 9.
16 Fricke, "U2 Finds What It's Looking For," *Rolling Stone*, October 1992, p. 48.
17 Bailie, *op. cit.*, p. 114.
18 McCormick, *op. cit.*, p. 280.
19 *Ibid.*, p. 281.
20 *Ibid.*, p. 278.
21 "Achtung Baby: Presented by The Edge and Adam Clayton," U2 X-Radio, November 24, 2021.
22 McCormick, *op. cit.*, p. 283.
23 Bailie, *op. cit.*, p. 115.
24 Hilburn, "U2's Pride (In the Name of Songs): Bono and Edge evaluate one critic's choices for the group's 10 best recordings, from 'I Will Follow' to 'One'," *Los Angeles Times*, September 12, 1993, www.latimes.com/archives/la-xpm-1993-09-12-ca-34478-story.html.
25 Flanagan, *op. cit.*, p. 63.

Chapter 8

1 Jackson, "Bono vs. The Beast ," *Musician*, August 1993, p. 30.
2 Wroe, "The Edge Of The Zoo," *Propaganda*, November 1993, No. 18, p. 5.
3 *Ibid.*, p. 7.
4 Flanagan, *At the End of the World* (1995), p. 185.
5 McCormick, *U2 by U2* (2009), p. 307.
6 Wroe, *op. cit.*, p. 7.
7 McCormick, *op. cit.*, p. 307.
8 Jackson, *op. cit.*, p. 32.
9 Turner, *The Man Called Cash*, 2005. p. 191.

Chapter 10

1 Brugger, *Max* magazine, April 1997, www.u2songs.com/news/pop_interview_with_max_magazine.
2 Cameron, "…Only now do we look cool," *NME Originals U2*, November 2002, p. 131.
3 "The Edge and Woody Harrelson Talk Pop," U2 X-Radio, October 12, 2020.
4 Wroe, "I can still hear the edits," *Propaganda*, Spring/Summer 1997, No. 26, p. 19.
5 U2, Interviewed by Jo Whiley, BBC Radio 1, March 1, 1997.
6 *Ibid.*
7 *Ibid.*
8 McCormick, *U2 by U2* (2009), p. 330.
9 Brugger, *op. cit.*
10 McCormick, "Growing Up with U2," *The Daily Telegraph*, January 1, 1997, www. telegraph.co.uk/main.jhtml?xml=/1997/03/01/bryutu01.xml.
11 U2, interviewed by Jo Whiley, BBC Radio 1, March 1, 1997.
12 Wroe, "U2 Go Pop," *Propaganda*, Winter 1997, No. 25, p. 11.
13 Doyle, "The Professionals," *Q* magazine, April 1997, p. 97.
14 Bono, interviewed by Dave Fanning, RTÉ Radio 2, February 20, 1997.
15 McCormick, *U2 by U2* (2009), p. 332.
16 *Ibid.*
17 Brugger, *op. cit.*
18 Stokes, "U2 Release Pop," *Hot Press*, April 3, 1997, www.hotpress.com/music/day-1997-u2-release-pop-22806910.

19 *Ibid.*
20 U2, interviewed by Jo Whiley, BBC Radio 1, March 1, 1997.
21 Wroe, "The Pop Issue," *Propaganda*, Spring/Summer 1997, No. 26, p. 16.
22 Tingen, "Producing U2's Pop," *Sound on Sound*, July 1997, www.soundonsound.com/people/flood-howie-b-producing-u2s-pop.
23 Wroe, "The Pop Issue," *Propaganda*, Spring/Summer 1997, No. 26, p. 16.
24 U2, Interviewed by Jo Whiley, BBC Radio 1, March 1, 1997.
25 McCormick, *U2 by U2* (2009), p. 334.
26 Bono, interviewed by Dave Fanning, RTÉ Radio 2, February 20, 1997.
27 *Ibid.*
28 *Ibid.*
29 Wroe, "The Pop Issue," *op. cit.*, p. 17.
30 Sams, "North and South of the River Single," U2Songs.com, retrieved December 17, 2021, www.u2songs.com/discography/moore_christy_bono_and_the_edge_north_and_south_of_the_river_single.

Chapter 11

1   Heath, "Band of the Year: U2" *Rolling Stone*, January 18, 2001, p. 39.
2   *Ibid.*
3   The Edge, "Stuck in a Moment You Can't Get Out Of" Promotional Release, 2000.
4   Michael Stipe and Mario Batalli, *Iconoclasts*, December 12, 2005.
5   Greene "U2's the Edge on 'All That You Can't Leave Behind' at 20: 'It Was a Natural Moment to Reboot'" *Rolling Stone*, October 23, 2020, www.rollingstone.com/music/music-features/u2-the-edge-interview-all-that-you-cant-leave-behind-1078907/.
6   U2, All That You Can't Leave Behind Promotional Tour, December 5, 2000, Irving Plaza, New York, NY.
7   Heath, *op. cit.*, p. 41.
8   Baltin, "Sunday Conversation: U2's Adam Clayton on 20 Years Of 'All That You Can't Leave Behind'" *Forbes*, December 6, 2020, www.forbes.com/sites/stevebaltin/2020/12/06/sunday-conversation-u2s-adam-clayton-on-20-years-of-all-that-you-cant-leave-behind-springsteen-growing-older-in-music-and-more/.
9   Heath, *op. cit.*, p. 39.
10 Wroe, "Hear and Now," *Propaganda*, Vol. 2, No. 2, p. 38.
11 Baltin, *op. cit.*
12 Eccleston, "The Elastic Bono Band," *Q* magazine, November 2000, p. 88.
13 Wroe, *op. cit.*, p. 38.
14 The Edge, "Stuck in a Moment You Can't Get Out Of" Promotional Release, 2000.
15 "Closer to the Edge (Part I)," *The Irish Times*, October 21, 2000, www.irishtimes.com/news/closer-to-the-edge-part-1-1.1111411.
16 Greene, "U2's the Edge on 'All That You Can't Leave Behind' at 20: 'It Was a Natural Moment to Reboot'" *Rolling Stone*, October 23, 2020, www.rollingstone.com/music/music-features/u2-the-edge-interview-all-that-you-cant-leave-behind-1078907/.
17 The Edge, "Stuck in a Moment You Can't Get Out Of" Promotional Release, 2000.
18 *Ibid.*
19 "Closer to the Edge (Part I)," *The Irish Times*, October 21, 2000, www.irishtimes.com/news/closer-to-the-edge-part-1-1.1111411.
20 McCormick, *U2 by U2* (2009), p. 337.
21 The Edge, "Stuck in a Moment You Can't Get Out Of" Promotional Release, 2000.
22 *Ibid.*
23 Greene, *op. cit.*
24 The Edge, "Stuck in a Moment You Can't Get Out Of" Promotional Release, 2000.
25 McCormick, *op. cit.*, p. 337.
26 "Sounds of Silence" *Sydney Morning Herald*, September 19, 2002, www.smh.com.au/entertainment/music/sounds-of-silence-20020919-gdfnb5.html.

Chapter 12

1   McCormick, *U2 by U2* (2009), p. 399.
2   Sams, "Shark Soup Demo," U2Songs.com, retrieved December 17, 2021, www.u2songs.com/demos/shark_soup.
3   McCormick, *op. cit.*, p. 403.
4   Lillywhite, "The Lillywhite Sessions," *East Village Radio*, November 17, 2009.
5   U2, *How to Dismantle an Atomic Bomb Interview Disc* Promotional Release, 2004.
6   Deevoy, "It Could Be About God," *Blender*, November 2004, p. 122.
7   "The Bomb Squad: U2's Track by Track Guide to How to Dismantle an Atomic Bomb," *Q* magazine, November 2004, p. 73.
8   "The Opera in Me," U2.com, December 14, 2004, www.u2.com/news/title/the-opera-in-me/.
9   "The Bomb Squad: U2's Track by Track Guide to How to Dismantle an Atomic Bomb," *Q* magazine, November 2004, p. 73.
10 Sams and Morgan, "City of Blinding Lights," U2Songs.com, retrieved December 17, 2021, www.u2songs.com/discography/u2_city_of_blinding_lights_single.
11 Deevoy, *op. cit.*, p. 122.
12 McCormick, *op. cit.*, p. 409.
13 "The Bomb Squad: U2's Track by Track Guide to How to Dismantle an Atomic Bomb," *Q* magazine, November 2004, p. 73.
14 Deevoy, *op. cit.*, p. 122.
15 "The Bomb Squad: U2's Track by Track Guide to How to Dismantle an Atomic Bomb," *Q* magazine, November 2004, p. 73.
16 "You Don't Have to Be Shy About It," U2.com, August 1, 2006, www.u2.com/news/title/you_dont_have_to_be_shy_about_it_1974.
17 "The Bomb Squad: U2's Track by Track Guide to How to Dismantle an Atomic Bomb," *Q* magazine, November 2004, p. 73.

Chapter 13

1   Corkill, "Photographer Sugimoto Strikes a Stone Age deal with U2," *The Japan Times*, March 20, 2009, www.japantimes.co.jp/culture/2009/03/20/arts/photographer-sugimoto-strikes-a-stone-age-deal-with-u2.
2   U2, interviewed by Simon Mayo, BBC Radio 5, February 27, 2009.
3   Doyle, "Did You Miss Us?," *Q* magazine, February 2009, p. 47.
4   Frenette, "'Futuristic spirituals': Daniel Lanois talks about recording the new U2 album," *National Post*, March 11, 2009, nationalpost.com/news/futuristic-spirituals-daniel-lanois-talks-about-recording-the-new-u2-album/.
5   Hiatt, "Exploring U2's Bold New 'Horizon'," *Rolling Stone*, March 9, 2009, www.rollingstone.com/news/story/25585554/inside_u2s_bold_new_horizon.
6   U2, *No Line on the Horizon* Liner Notes, 2009.
7   Frenette, *op. cit.*
8   Hiatt, *op. cit.*
9   O'Hagan, "The Wanderers," *The Guardian*, February 15, 2009, www.theguardian.com/music/2009/feb/15/u2-no-line-on-the-horizon.
10 *Ibid.*
11 U2, interviewed by Jo Whiley, "Live Lounge," BBC Radio 1, February 27, 2009.
12 Larry Mullen, interviewed by Larry Gogan, RTÉ 2FM, March 8, 2009.
13 Frenette, *op. cit.*
14 Hiatt, *op. cit.*
15 U2, interviewed by Jo Whiley, "Live Lounge," BBC Radio 1, February 27, 2009.
16 Doyle, *op. cit.*, p. 44.
17 Bono and The Edge, interviewed by Christian O'Connell, Absolute Radio, February 26, 2009.

18 "Will.i.am. Borrowed Melody From U2 Song," *Contact Music*, April 20, 2012, www.contactmusic.com/jimmy-iovine/news/william-borrowed-melody-from-u2-song_1320653.
19 O'Hagan, *op. cit.*
20 U2, interviewed by John Wilson, "Front Row," BBC Radio 4, February 24, 2009.
21 Frenette, *op. cit.*
22 Wroughton, "Poverty campaign inspires new U2 song, says Bono," Reuters, October 22, 2008, www.reuters.com/article/idINIndia-36108120081023.
23 Frenette, *op. cit.*
24 O'Hagan, *op. cit.*
25 Frenette, *op. cit.*
26 U2, interviewed by John Wilson, "Front Row," BBC Radio 4, February 24, 2009.
27 Larry Mullen, interviewed by Larry Gogan, RTÉ 2FM, March 8, 2009.
28 Frenette, *op. cit.*
29 The Edge, interviewed by Ian Camfield, XFM Radio, March 2, 2009.
30 U2, interviewed by John Wilson, "Front Row," BBC Radio 4, February 24, 2009.
31 U2, interviewed by Jo Whiley, "Live Lounge," BBC Radio 1, February 27, 2009.
32 *Ibid.*
33 Frenette, *op. cit.*
34 U2, interviewed by John Wilson, "Front Row," BBC Radio 4, February 24, 2009.

Chapter 14

1 Wenner, "Exclusive: Bono Reveals Secrets of U2's Surprise Album 'Songs of Innocence'," *Rolling Stone*, September 9, 2014, www.rollingstone.com/music/music-news/exclusive-bono-reveals-secrets-of-u2s-surprise-album-songs-of-innocence-106257/.
2 "Songs of Innocence," *U2.com*, September 9, 2014, www.u2.com/news/title/songs-of-innocence/16/14.
3 Hiatt "Exploring U2's Bold New 'Horizon'," *Rolling Stone*, March 9, 2009, www.rollingstone.com/news/story/25585554/inside_u2s_bold_new_horizon.
4 Hiatt "U2: Trying to Throw Their Arms Around the World," *Rolling Stone*, May 15, 2015, www.rollingstone.com/music/music-news/u2-trying-to-throw-their-arms-around-the-world-46041/.
5 Wenner, *op. cit.*
6 *Ibid.*
7 *Ibid.*
8 Bono, interviewed by Dave Fanning, RTÉ 2FM, September 21, 2014.
9 *Ibid.*
10 *Ibid.*
11 *Ibid.*
12 Lynskey, "U2: 'It's the job of art to be divisive'," *The Guardian*, October 12, 2014, www.theguardian.com/music/2014/oct/12/u2-job-art-divisive-interview.
13 *Ibid.*
14 *Ibid.*
15 Walsh, "Bono Reveals Inspiration Behind U2's New Album," *Irish Central*, September 14, 2014, www.irishcentral.com/culture/entertainment/bono-reveals-inspiration-behind-u2s-new-album.
16 Bono and The Edge, "U2 - Cedarwood Road ," *Song Exploder* Podcast, June 2015.
17 Bono and The Edge, interviewed by Hrishikesh Hirway, "U2 - Cedarwood Road ," *Song Exploder* Podcast, June 2015.
18 U2, *Innocence + Experience: Live in Paris*, 2016.
19 Walsh, "Bono Reveals Inspiration Behind U2's New Album," *Irish Central*, September 14, 2014, www.irishcentral.com/culture/entertainment/bono-reveals-inspiration-behind-u2s-new-album.
20 Bono, interviewed by Dave Fanning, RTÉ 2FM, September 21, 2014.
21 "Gavin Friday Presents," U2 X-Radio, October 8, 2021.
22 Bono, interviewed by Dave Fanning, RTÉ 2FM, September 21, 2014.

23 Lynskey, *op. cit.*

24 "This is About Songs," U2.com, September 23, 2014, www.u2.com/news/title/this-is-about-songs/u.

25 Newman, "9 Biggest Relevations in Bono's 'BBC' Interview About U2," *Rolling Stone*, February 4, 2014, www.rollingstone.com/music/music-news/9-biggest-revelations-in-bonos-bbc-interview-about-u2-172174/.

26 U2, Innocence + Experience Tour, June 29, 2015, United Center, Chicago, IL.

Chapter 15

1   Greene, "Bono on How U2's 'Songs of Experience' Evolved, Taking on Donald Trump," *Rolling Stone*, September 20, 2017, www.rollingstone.com/music/music-features/bono-on-how-u2s-songs-of-experience-evolved-taking-on-donald-trump-253312/.

2   Sams, "Love is All We Have Left Demo" U2Songs.com, retrieved December 21, 2021, www.u2songs.com/demos/love_is_all_we_have_left.

3   Greene, "Bono on How U2's 'Songs of Experience' Evolved," *op. cit.*

4   Sams, "Euromantic Remix: An Interview with Jon Pleased Wimmin," U2Songs.com, March 2, 2019, www.u2songs.com/news/euromantic_remixes_an_interview_with_jon_pleased_wimmin.

5   Dean, "Bono on death, taxes and their new album Songs of Experience," *The Times*, November 19, 2017, www.thetimes.co.uk/article/u2-interview-bono-paradise-papers-taxes-new-album-songs-of-experience-hsf7sf25k.

6   Eamon Dunphy, interviewed by Ray D'Arcy, RTÉ 2FM, May 20, 2017.

7   Sams, "You're the Best Thing About Me (New York Video)," U2Songs.com, retrieved December 21, 2021, www.u2songs.com/videos/youre_the_best_thing_about_me.

8   Sams, "Love is Bigger: Will Clarke Interview," U2Songs.com, May 16, 2018, www.u2songs.com/news/love_is_bigger_will_clarke_interview.

9   Yoo, "U2's New Video Depicts the KKK at the White House," Pitchfork.com, January 18, 2018, pitchfork.com/news/u2s-new-video-depicts-the-kkk-at-the-white-house/.

10 Sams, "The Missing Amsterdam Video for 'You're The Best Thing About Me'," U2Songs.com, July 29, 2019, www.u2songs.com/news/the_missing_amsterdam_video_for_youre_the_best_thing_about_me.

11 Bono, interviewed by Lin Brehmer, WXRT Radio, September 6, 2017.

12 Greene, "The Edge on U2's 'Songs of Experience,' Bono's 'Brush With Mortality," *Rolling Stone*, September 18, 2017, www.rollingstone.com/music/music-features/the-edge-on-u2s-songs-of-experience-bonos-brush-with-mortality-253290/.

13 Bono and The Edge, interviewed by Dave Fanning, RTÉ 2FM, December 16, 2017.

14 *Ibid.*

15 Doyle, "Blake Expectations," *MOJO* magazine, April 2017, p. 84.

16 Lynskey, "Where the Magic Happens," *Q* magazine, October 2015, p. 39.

17 Greene, "Bono on How U2's 'Songs of Experience' Evolved," *op. cit.*

18 Gundersen, "Bono Honored as 2003 MusiCares Person of the Year," *Grammy* magazine, February 20, 2003.

19 "Music Can Pull People Together…," U2.com, January 12, 2017, www.u2.com/news/title/music-can-pull-people-together/news/.

20 Bono, interviewed by Eoghan McDermott, RTÉ 2FM, November 5, 2017.

21 Bureau, "Bono's Edge of Reason," *The Telegraph India*, December 1, 2017, www.telegraphindia.com/entertainment/bonoas-edge-of-reason-190035.

22 *Ibid.*

23 *Ibid.*

24 Bono, interviewed by Bill Flanagan, "Written in My Soul," SiriusXM Radio, October 18, 2017.

25 Willman, "Bono and 'Sing 2' Director Garth Jennings on How They Breathed Emotion Into a Guitar-Slinging Lion," *Variety*, December 3, 2021, variety.com/2021/music/musicians/bono-garth-jennings-sing-2-u2-1235124980/.

Bibliography

Books

Flanagan, B., *At the End of the World* (New York: Delacorte Press, 1995)
McCormick, N., *U2 by U2* (New York: It Books, 2009)
Stokes, N., *U2 In the Name of Love: A History from Ireland's Hot Press Magazine* (New York: Harmony Books, 1985)
Stokes, N., *U2: Into the Heart* (New York: Thunder's Mouth Press, 2002)
Stokes, N., *Three Chords and the Truth* (New York: Harmony Books, 1989)
Turner, S., *The Man Called Cash: The Life, Love and Faith of an American Legend* (Nashville: Thomas Nelson, 2005)
Waters, J., *Race of Angels: The Genesis of U2* (London: Fourth Estate, 1994)

Magazines

Billboard (USA, 1894–Present)
Blender (USA, 1994–2009)
Creem Collectors Series (USA, 1969–1989)
Forbes magazine (USA, 1917–Present)
GQ magazine (USA, 1931–Present)
History of Rock (UK, 2015–2017)
Hit Parader (USA, 1942–2008)
Hot Press magazine (Ireland, 1977–Present)
Grammy magazine (USA)
Maclean's (Canada, 1905–Present)
Max magazine (France, 1989–2006)
MOJO magazine (1993–Present)
Musician magazine (USA, 1976–1999)
New Musical Express (NME) (UK, 1952–Present)
NME Originals (UK, 2002–Present)
Propaganda magazine (UK, 1986–2001)
Q magazine (UK, 1986–2020)
Rolling Stone (USA, 1967–Present)
Sound on Sound (UK, 1985–Present)
Spin (USA, 1985–Present)
U2 Magazine (UK, 1982–1985)

Newspapers

The Daily Journal (Franklin, IN, USA), *The Daily Telegraph* (London, England), *The Irish Times* (Dublin, Ireland), *The Japan Times* (Tokyo, Japan), *The Guardian* (London, England), *Los Angeles Times* (Los Angeles, CA, USA), *National Post* (Toronto, ON, Canada), *The New York Times* (New York, NY, USA), *Sydney Morning Herald* (Sydney, Australia), *The Telegraph India* (Kolkata, India)

Other News Media

Absolute Radio, BBC Radio, Contact Music, East Village Radio, Iconoclasts (TV), Island Records Press Release, Irish Central, NRJ Radio, Piccadilly Radio, Radio Today, Reuters, Rockline Radio, Rock and Roll Hall of Fame, RTÉ Radio 2, Song Exploder Podcast, U2 X-Radio, WXRT Radio, XFM Radio.

Sleeve Notes/Recordings

Another Time, Another Place (2015)
October Liner Notes (2008)
"Stuck in a Moment" Promotional Release (2001)
No Line on the Horizon Liner Notes (2009)

Websites

U2Songs.com www.u2songs.com
U2.com www.u2.com